Welsh Canoe Classics

A CANOEIST AND KAYAKER'S GUIDE

Eddie Palmer, Adam Robson
& Nigel Wilford

First published in Great Britain 2016 by Pesda Press
Tan y Coed Canol
Ceunant
Caernarfon
Gwynedd
LL55 4RN

© Copyright 2016 Eddie Palmer, Adam Robson & Nigel Wilford

ISBN: 978-1-906095-55-0

Maps – Bute Cartographic
Contains Ordnance Survey Data © Crown copyright and database right 2016
Printed in Poland, www.lfbookservices.co.uk

Dedication

This book is dedicated to Wilf's father, Trevor David Wilford, who died of pancreatic cancer 14 October 2016, aged 71.

For information on pancreatic cancer visit www.pancreaticcanceraction.org

Contents

Important Notice – Disclaimer

Canoeing and kayaking are healthy outdoor activities that carry some degree of risk. They involve adventurous travel, often away from close habitation. Guidebooks give an idea of where to access a river, where to egress, the level of difficulty and the nature of the hazards to be encountered.

However, nature being what it is, river valleys are changed by time and erosion, water levels vary considerably with rain, and man-made features can be updated or altered – therefore weirs, walls and landings are not always as expected. Coastal sections, large lakes and estuaries are also subject to change due to wind and weather. This guidebook is no substitute for personal inspection at the time of paddling, and your own risk assessment and judgement. Your decision to paddle or not, and any consequences arising from that decision, is your responsibility.

Introduction

Welcome to Welsh Canoe Classics – a collection of the best rivers, lakes, canals and coastal trips in Wales compiled by the three authors, all experienced canoeists. This is not a guide to all canoeing rivers in Wales, but to the ones the authors have enjoyed most, whether for the water, the scenery, the interesting surroundings, or nearby attractions. This guide will be most useful to beginners and moderate paddlers, and aims to provide a selection of enjoyable trips, most of which can be paddled with loaded open canoes.

One difference from the other books in the 'Canoe Classics' series is that it includes a few smaller and higher grade rivers which, although usually paddled in a kayak, have become accessible to open canoeists in recent years as their skill levels have increased. These rivers would, however, be difficult with loaded canoes. We have marked them with (WW) – 'whitewater' after the title and with the symbol of the appropriate grade.

The regional divisions are ours, and seem to make sense.

Acknowledgements

From Eddie – Thanks to all my paddling friends over the years, particularly those who took me, as a gawky teenager, on my first moving water in the Midlands, and then on to whitewater in North Wales. They are too many to mention. Thanks also to all the people I met on the recent expeditions in Wales. Most were very friendly and helpful. Also to Ellie for her patience.

From Adam – Many thanks, in a new endeavour for me, to Jimmy Mitchell, Paul Maton, Tim Vercoe, Chris Leesmith, Colin Crockart, Richard Witheridge and Paul Morrissey.

From 'Wilf' – There are so many people to thank, not just for their assistance with the production of this book, but for their help in general. To my wife Ruth, and our children Emily and Dominic, thank you for sharing my passion for boating and adventures, your enthusiasm and tolerance is so important. For the endless encouragement and support from the rest of my family and to all of you who have paddled with me, helped explore new routes, had your photograph taken, driven to places to pick me up or looked after my family while I've been elsewhere, a most sincere, thank you.

All three of us have to thank Ray Goodwin for various bits of help and encouragement over the years!

The photographs were taken by the authors, unless otherwise indicated.

The Authors

Eddie Palmer

Eddie's first kayak, over 50 years ago, was made from wood and canvas, He set out in it to paddle rivers in his part of middle England and Wales. Since then, he has kayaked and canoed extensively in the UK, Ireland, Western and Eastern Europe, the USA, Canada, and Southern Africa. Eddie has also competed in slalom and whitewater racing and continues to paddle whitewater. He is also a sailor. His passion over the past few years has been long-distance canoe camping journeys.

Eddie is a Board Director of the Scottish Canoe Association. He is the author of *Scottish Canoe Classics* and the co-author of *Scottish Canoe Touring, Irish Canoe Classics, English Canoe Classics – North* and *English Canoe Classics – South*.

Adam Robson

Adam (or Robson as he is more commonly known) is an experienced paddler and paddlesport coach and guide. He began his paddling career in the Scouts, where he developed an interest in both freestyle kayaking and descending whitewater rivers. As his knowledge and skills developed, so did his ambitions. Adam has paddled many of the favourite whitewater runs in England, Wales, Scotland and the Alps. Having experienced coaching in the early stages of his paddling life and recognising its benefits, Adam joined the British Canoe Union (BCU) Coaching Service to share his enthusiasm, aid the development of others, and become a respected river leader.

His interest in canoeing started one dry summer when he borrowed an old open canoe on the River Dee at Llangollen. His curiosity turned into a passion and he purposefully set out to master the craft, exploring its intricacies and versatility. During this personal journey he has completed several solo, unsupported long-distance expeditions in the UK and Europe including Wales' River Dee source to sea trip.

Nigel Wilford

Nigel has been involved with canoeing for most of his adult life, paddling throughout the UK, mainland Europe, Canada, USA and New Zealand. Born in North West Leicestershire, his first canoe experience was on the gentle River Soar. Not long after, he moved to Yorkshire to attend university. The enjoyment he found while paddling the rivers of the North East firmly established canoeing as his activity of choice. In 1991 he joined the BCU Coaching Service, helping others to improve their canoeing or to become better coaches.

Nigel has held various roles within the BCU including Local Coaching Organiser and English White Water Safety Coordinator. He is a BCU (now British Canoeing) Level 5 Coach and brand ambassador for Pyranha. Nigel is also the co-author of *English Canoe Classics – North* and *English Canoe Classics South*.

Using the Guide

To use the guide, you will need an up-to-date and appropriate Ordnance Survey map of the relevant area and the ability to use it. In addition, for any tidal area you will need up-to-date tide tables.

Each route begins with some quick reference information, relevant Ordnance Survey (OS) Landranger 1:50,000 maps, length of the route in kilometres, vehicle shuttle distances, portages and start and finish points. This is followed by an overall description of the area, details of access points and water levels, and finally a route description with distances between the main features.

TYPES OF WATER

 Canals, slow-moving rivers and small inland lakes which are placid water, and easy to cope with.

 Inland lakes, still with no current or tide, but which in high winds can produce large waves.

 Rivers of a whitewater nature, or where flood conditions can make paddling difficult, and requiring a higher level of skill. The grade of any rapids is denoted from 1 to 4 within the icon.

 Estuaries, where the direction of the tide is all-important, and usually cannot be paddled against.

 Open sea, safer coastal routes suitable for placid water touring kayaks and canoes (in calm, stable weather).

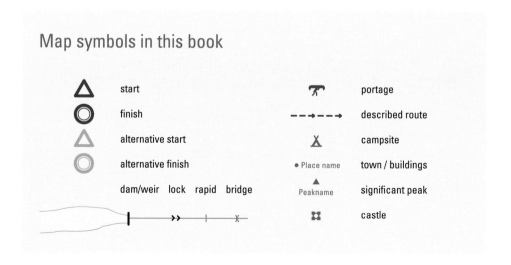

Map symbols in this book

△	start	🦫	portage
◎	finish	– – → – – →	described route
△	alternative start	✕	campsite
◎	alternative finish	• Place name	town / buildings
	dam/weir lock rapid bridge	▲ Peakname	significant peak
		♯	castle

RIVER GRADES

This book includes whitewater paddling of up to Grade 3 with a few portageable sections of Grade 4. Rivers are graded by the international river grading system from Grade 1 to Grade 6:

GRADE 1   Easy. Occasional small rapids or riffles, waves regular and low. Most appropriate course, with deepest water, easy to see from canoe or kayak and to steer down. Obstacles such as pebble banks very easy to see. Presents no problems to paddlers able to steer canoes and kayaks. Steering is needed, especially on narrow rivers.

GRADE 2   Medium. Fairly frequent rapids, usually with regular waves, easy eddies, and small whirlpools and boils. Course generally easy to recognise, but may meander around gravel banks and trees etc. Paddlers in kayaks may get wet, those in open canoes much less so.

GRADE 3   Difficult. Rapids numerous, and can be continuous. Course more difficult to see, landing to inspect may be wise. Drops may be high enough not to see water below, with high and irregular waves, broken water, eddies and whirlpools/boils. There is no water with rapids of above Grade 3 advised in this guide. Where there are Grade 3 rapids, avoiding or portaging is possible.

GRADE 4   Very difficult. Long and extended stretches of rapids with high, irregular waves, difficult broken water, strong eddies and whirlpools. Course often difficult to recognise. High falls, inspection from bank nearly always necessary.

GRADE 5   Exceedingly difficult. Long and unbroken stretches of whitewater with individual features, and routes very difficult to see. Many submerged rocks, high waterfalls, falls in steps, very difficult whirlpools and very fast eddies. Previous inspection absolutely necessary, risk of injury, swims always serious.

GRADE 6   Absolute limit of difficulty. Definite risk to life.

CAMPSITES

In the river sections, we have sometimes referred to specific sites, usually because they are actually on the river. Please note however that campsites can come and go, or change, for instance from taking tents to only taking caravans. For these reasons, we strongly urge readers to carry out an internet search for open campsites before setting off.

RIVER LEVEL

Getting the river level right is very important. Too low and the trip will be a scrape, too high and the river changes into a dangerous torrent. To help you determine the best level at which to paddle, we have suggested a variety of tools. For some rivers, it is simply a case of observing the water height from the road, a bridge, or checking a physical gauge in the river. For others, we have recommended websites where the data is easy to read.

www.rainchasers.com has been developed by Rob Tuley with information contributed by paddlers. The site uses Environment Agency/Natural Resources Wales data available under Open Government Licence.

www.riverlevels.uk is an independent website providing river level information using Environment Agency/Natural Resources Wales data available under Open Government Licence.

https://flood-warning-information.service.gov.uk is a service provided by the UK Government which covers Welsh rivers which flow into England. Select 'View the latest river and sea levels near you' and don't be put off by 'Enter a place or postcode in England'. It will work for the rivers where we have recommended it.

Flood monitoring in Wales is the responsibility of Natural Resources Wales (NRW – Cyfoeth Naturiol Cymru in Welsh). Unfortunately at the time of going to print the NRW 'river levels' webpage is still under construction. Natural Resources Wales was created a few years ago by merging the Environment Agency, the Forestry Commission and the Countryside Council for Wales.

Please use the system sensibly and cautiously. Make sure that the data you are looking at is relevant. Major rivers, for instance the Teifi, have several measuring stations, so make sure you are reading levels where you might actually paddle! As a general rule of thumb, the best (and safest) level to paddle will be towards the top end of the typical range. If it says 'flooding is possible', the river will be going over its banks and this is probably not a good time to launch your canoe. Wales has some very 'flashy' rivers in steep valleys, that rise very fast, and an extra metre of water can easily materialise in a few hours (or even minutes).

ACCESS IN WALES

This is our personal understanding of the situation at the time of writing in 2016. These notes are written without prejudice.

Canoeists in England and Wales do not enjoy unequivocal access arrangements to all inland waters. This means that on occasions land owners may not wish to have people journeying through their land. The routes included in this book have all been paddled free from significant access impediments, for many years. However, the situation may change and canoeists are strongly advised to check the access situation before embarking upon a trip.

The latest legal opinion, by the Rev. Douglas Caffyn, PhD, is that there has never been an act of parliament which rescinded the original rights of access and navigation on all rivers. To date, no legal adverse opinion or court judgement is being sought to challenge this opinion.

No canoeist has ever been taken to court for 'trespassing' on a river in England or Wales, and 'trespass' is a breach of the civil rights of the owner, not a police matter. One day we hope to secure a fair and unambiguous arrangement for access to all of our waterways. Until then canoeists must anticipate that they may be challenged about the legitimacy of their presence on our beautiful rivers. This advice does not entitle you to recklessly interrupt angling, or disturb spawning ground in autumn or winter.

Some years ago, Canoe Wales, the governing body for paddling in Wales, decided to stop giving 'access advice' to individuals or clubs. Their thinking was that by doing so, they were colluding with restricting people's rights of access to water. There are a few helpful local paddlers ready to give people advice, but the lack of a centralised 'access system' has resulted in an unhelpful 'free-for-all', with paddlers going wherever they can.

The Welsh Government has consulted on the issue, and made some moves to increase access to land, but unfortunately it has shied away from legislating about water. A Welsh Government consultation in mid-2015 said, 'we encourage more voluntary access agreements', but it doesn't look as if this is helping matters. Canoe Wales responded to this consultation.

We strongly recommend membership of Canoe Wales, particularly for the automatic third party insurance cover which is essential for anybody undertaking outdoor activities.

An introduction to canoeing – finding instruction

Paddling a canoe or a kayak can bring great pleasure and does not require large financial resources. However, simply buying a craft and heading for the nearest water can quickly turn an afternoon out into an epic. Most canoeists who get into trouble have the right gear but no idea about how to use it, and are unaware of their surrounding environment.

It is essential that you learn not only how to paddle efficiently, but also how to organise a trip and take into account factors such as water height and flow, tide, wind and weather. Experienced paddlers may cover 30 miles a day on some rivers but novices will not be able to. Paddling in company, rather than by yourself, is much safer.

If you are not an experienced canoeist, please seek instruction from a local canoe club, a centre with approved coaches, or approach your national governing body for advice on getting started. In Wales, information is available from www.canoewales.com.

WEIRS

Please note – some of the rivers in this book feature weirs. Do not shoot them unless confident of your competence and ability to assess the risk involved.

PORTAGES

'Portaging' means 'carrying boats and supplies overland' and is taken from the French 'portage', 'to carry'. Portaging is often necessary to cross weirs and locks. The portages mentioned in this book are usually about 50 metres long, but in a few rare cases can be much longer, and will require both boat and gear to be carried.

On flat ground, a canoe trolley may be useful. A good quality, sturdy and long-lasting trolley will cost £70–£100 and is an investment that we thoroughly recommend.

USING THE INTERNET

Maps and satellite images found on the internet are useful resources to familiarise yourself with areas you intend to paddle. 'Google Earth' images can be used to follow the whole course of a river to identify weirs and other dangers. There are also various online mapping programmes derived from the British Ordnance Survey (OS) system. It is a good idea to take either a paper OS map or a printed page off the internet (make it waterproof!) with you.

Online information can also be useful for planning shuttles and identifying rendezvous points. The access and egress points for the trips included in this book have been chosen for their proximity to easy parking for vehicles, but it is worth double-checking them before embarking on a long journey.

ENVIRONMENTAL CONCERNS FOR CANOEISTS

Paddlers have a duty to do their best to keep our environment clean and tidy. This includes not dropping litter, but maybe also, in a community-spirited way, cleaning up after other people. The main areas needing care are when camping in the wild, and preventing the transfer of non-native invasive species from one river system to another.

Where available, paddlers should always use formal campsites. In Wales, wild camping requires the consent of the landowner, and is therefore more appropriate in the wilder areas of Scotland and Ireland.

Winter paddle on the Mawddach Estuary | Ray Goodwin

NORTH WEST WALES

River Conwy – wooded upper reaches

North West Wales

North West Wales, for the purpose of this book, includes the counties of Gwynedd and Conwy. This is the part of Wales which boasts the highest mountains in the principality, and as a consequence, the fastest rivers, which fall rapidly to the sea.

The area is compact and varied. Snowdon, the highest mountain in Wales, dominates and on clear days, the views from the summit extend across the Irish Sea to Ireland. A historic mountain railway climbs all the way to the top. Snowdonia National Park offers an extensive network of trails, over a hundred lakes, and craggy peaks including Cadair Idris and Tryfan. To the north-west, the land slopes away to the Menai Strait and the Isle of Anglesey twenty miles away, a great sea kayaking destination. To the west lies the scenic Lleyn Peninsula, and a mere twelve miles to the south, Tremadog and the lovely sandy beaches stretching down to Cardigan Bay.

East of Snowdon, Betws-y-Coed nestles at the head of the Conwy Valley and down-stream, Conwy Castle guards the mouth of the river. The seaside resorts of Llandudno and Colwyn Bay are nearby.

The entire area can get very busy during peak holidays as it attracts walkers, climbers and many canoeists.

The Origins of Gwynedd

Gwynedd (pronounced 'gwyneth' in Welsh) was an independent kingdom from the end of the Roman period until the 13th century when it was conquered by England. The modern Gwynedd was one of eight Welsh counties created in 1974; its area was based on the principal territory of the former realm. It covered the entirety of the old counties of Anglesey and Caernarvonshire along with most of Merionethshire. Later Anglesey became a county in its own right.

Although Gwynedd is the second largest county in Wales, it is sparsely populated with around 122,000 inhabitants. Two-thirds of the population speak Welsh, with an even higher proportion of 94% among school children.

📷 Conwy Harbour

River Conwy near Llanrwst

01 River Conwy

 **OS Sheets 115 & 116 or OL17** | **Llanrwst to Deganwy** | **22km**

Shuttle	14 miles via A55 and A470, 25min
Start	Llanrwst, upstream of the bridge, river left, SH 799 613
Finish	Deganwy public pontoon and slipway, SH 777 791

Introduction

Flowing from Lake Conwy on the Migneint, a large area of moorland, the River Conwy winds its way north, passing Betws-y-Coed, Llanrwst and the town of Conwy itself before emptying into the Irish Sea.

The Conwy is all things to all men; the upper reaches are classic intermediate white-water, the infamous Fairy Glen is a test piece of Welsh grade 5, while the lower section, described below, offers stunning scenic touring starting in the Vale of Conwy and finishing at the seaside. The trip is best done in glorious sunshine with a light south-westerly wind.

This route is in the most attractive part of North Wales. In addition to the delights of the upper valley and the pretty village of Betws-y-Coed, the end of the trip takes in

N

Great Orme's Head/
Pen-y-Gogarth

Llandudno

Penrhyn Bay

Conwy Bay/
Bae Conwy

Llanrhos

Colwyn Bay

Llandudno
Junction

Aberg

A470

A55

Conwy

A547

Penmaenmawr

A55

Bryn-y-maen

B5383

Glan Conwy

Llanfairfechan

B5381

Dolwen

Betws-yn-Rhos

Abergwyngregyn

B5106

B5381

B1040

Moelfre
Uchaf

Ty'n-y-groes

Tal-y-cefn

B5113

Llanfair Talhaiarn

Foel-Fras

Tal-y-Bont

Mwdwl
Eithin

Pentre Isaf

Drosgl

Dulyn
Reservoir

Dolgarrog

Llangernyw

Llansannan

Carnedd
Llewelyn

Llyn
Eigiau
Reservoir

B5106

A548

Pandy Tudur

B5384

arnedd
Dafydd

Ffynnon
Llugwy
Reservoir

Llyn
Cowlyd
Reservoir

Trefriw

Llanddoged

Pentre-tafarn
-y-fedw

Gwytherin

Llanrwst

Moel Llyn

Llyn
Crafnant
Reservoir

Afon Llugwy

A5

Moel
Seisiog

Llyn Aled

Capel Curig

A5

Nebo

Llyn Alwen

A4086

Pont Cyfyng

Carnedd
Moel-siabod

Betws-y-Coed

Llyn Elsi
Reservoir

B5113

A543

Hafod-Dinbych

Alw
Reser

Pont-y-pant

A470

Pentre-bont

Glan Conwy

Pentrefoelas

Rhydlydan

A5

Glasfryn

Penmachno

Afon Machno

Afon Conwy

Ysbyty Ifan

Moel
Penamnen

Pen y Bedw

Llyn
Conwy

Garn Prys

Carnedd
y Filiast

Blaenau Ffestiniog

B4407

0   4k

the magnificent Conwy Castle, and nearby, Llandudno and the Great Orme offer every holiday attraction one could ask for.

The traffic around Conwy can be busy in the summer, especially at weekends. It may be worth considering using the train for your shuttle; Deganwy Station is fifty metres from the finish, and a half hour train journey and ten minutes' walk gets you back to your car in Llanrwst. The service only runs every few hours, so do check times before committing to this.

Water level

This trip can be run all year round. A couple of sections may prove to be a scrape when the river is low, but otherwise the river is wide and deep.

The tides will play a big part in the timing of your trip; the river is tidal as far up as Trefriw, although exceptional spring tides have been known to reach Llanrwst. This far upriver there is a delay from the tide times published for the town of Conwy. Put on the water within the two hours following high water (HW) at Conwy and you will enjoy the assistance of the current in the upper reaches and the tide lower down. Any later than this and you risk grounding on the sand banks in the lower reaches.

High water at Conwy is Holyhead HW +0030; low water at Conwy is Holyhead LW +0110. If using a Dover tide table, high water at Conwy is Dover HW -0010.

Campsites

There are no campsites on the river. Erw Glas Campsite is about halfway along the shuttle near Dolgarrog. There are plenty of camping and caravan parks around Conwy and several sites towards Betws-y-Coed.

Access and egress

Start in Llanrwst – park in the car park by the rugby club. Walk across the small park, past the stone circle, to the river (SH 799 613). Launch upstream of the bridge, river left.

Finish in Deganwy – there is a public pontoon and slipway almost at the mouth of the estuary on the right bank (SH 777 791).

Description

Put on directly above Pont Fawr (Welsh for 'Big Bridge'), a 17th-century triple-arched stone bridge. The water here is fast moving even in low flow, so groups will often collect downstream of the bridge in an eddy, river right.

The river flows north out of town and a couple of straightforward shingle rapids are encountered. To the west, wooded hills overlook the valley. Before long a suspension bridge carrying a footpath is reached, and thereafter the railway is present on the right-hand side.

A double meander signals the approach of the village of Trefriw, the normal tidal limit of the Conwy.

More farmland and reed banks follow and after 2km you will pass under a private bridge near Dolgarrog (the finish for the 15km 'Conwy Ascent' annual race upstream, organised by Dyffryn Conwy Paddlers). Now you know exactly how far you have left to go.

The river starts to show signs of its tidal nature; a few sandbar islands, muddy banks and an increase in width. The tide will also start to play a major part in your progress, assuming you've timed it correctly. The cliffs above Coed y Borthol on the right bank become visible.

Several kilometres further along, the river narrows and there are cliffs on the left. This is Tal-y-cafn rapid, a 400m reminder that you are on a river. Catch an eddy up against the cliffs to peer into a dark cave; it takes little to imagine a Welsh dragon living here!

Shortly after, the river passes under a girder bridge carrying a minor road. Then, following a couple of bends, the river really starts to open out and you get the full sense of being in an estuary. Careful study of an OS map will help you stay in the channel and avoid the sand banks. The large village of Glan Conwy comes into view, river right, and you are into the final leg. Paddle around a huge left-hand bend and Conwy Castle is suddenly upon you. The water increases in speed and you pass under three bridges in close succession to emerge into the harbour in the shadow of the castle. Look out for Wales' smallest house on the left-hand side. Be sure to avoid the moored boats!

It is best to make your way over to the right bank toward the marina wall, and then follow the shoreline around, admiring the many boats. Just before the estuary narrows, take out behind Deganwy railway station up the public slipway.

Once changed, you can take full advantage of Deganwy's tourist facilities; a brew and an ice cream in the café opposite the station, or a visit to 'Harbour View Fish & Chips' just down the road is highly recommended.

Variation

The harbour itself is worth exploring and a few hours can easily be spent just taking in the sights, enjoying a unique view of the castle and paddling a short way up river. Launch at Deganwy an hour before high tide at Conwy; this should give you at least two hours of slack water. A short session here at slack water would make an ideal introduction to estuary paddling for children and adults alike.

Night falls – Llyn Padarn

 Moody Llyn Padarn

02 Llyn Padarn

OS Sheet 115 | **Round trip** | **7km**

Start	National Slate Museum, SH 583 605
Finish	National Slate Museum, SH 583 605

Introduction

Llyn Padarn is situated close to Llanberis, famous as the home of Welsh climbing with the Snowdon rock massifs and other nearby crags.

This is a very tourist-friendly part of Wales, with many attractions. The A55 is the gateway; to the Menai Strait, Anglesey, the university city of Bangor and the town of Caernarfon with yet another magnificent castle. Betws-y-Coed and the Conwy Valley are less than 20 miles to the east.

Padarn is a natural lake formed by a moraine lip at the northern end which holds the water in the valley and gives the lake its ribbon-like shape. It is just over three kilometres long and covers an area of about 250 acres. It has been designated an official freshwater bathing lake because of the cleanliness of the water, and is great for sailing, rowing and

LLYN PADARN

canoeing, but powered craft are banned. It was the venue for the 1958 Commonwealth Games rowing competition. Overlooked by Snowdon from the south and the peaks of the Glyders to the north-east, it offers a unique perspective on the mountains of Snowdonia.

The Gwynedd Council-owned country park at the southern end is well-known for its flora, with a great variety of trees and plants, many of them alpine. The park has five themed woodland trails and a special sessile oak woodland, Coed Dinorwig/Allt Wen, which is carefully preserved.

The National Slate Museum is well worth a visit. It was once the workshop for the vast Dinorwig Quarry which dominates the landscape to the east; this was one of the largest slate quarries in the world. Entry is free and there is a whole host of exhibits relating to the slate industry across Wales.

The area merits the 'five stars' awarded on Trip Advisor for the landscape, the scenery, the woodland, and the quiet of the lake! I cannot think of a better place to enjoy a summer's day splashing around in a canoe!

Campsites

There are many in the area. You could try Llwyn Celyn Bach www.campingllanberis.com.

Access and egress

Park in the pay and display car park by the National Slate Museum and follow the paths past the old mining buildings to the small lagoon. Launch here and paddle under the footbridge into the main body of the lake.

Description

The route is described anticlockwise. Turn right after exiting the lagoon. Paddle around the slate beach and follow the forested shoreline heading north-west. The narrow-gauge Llanberis Lake Railway follows the shoreline. Built in the 1840s, it was used to transport slate from the quarries to a small port on the Menai Strait; today it runs from Llanberis to the north end of the lake.

On the right is Coed Allt Wen, an ancient oak woodland and a Site of Special Scientific Interest.

About halfway along the lake narrows, and after it opens out again there is a greater sense of remoteness as Llanberis is hidden from view. The woodland gives way to rocky outcrops and there are several nice places to stop for a picnic. At the head of the lake, the Afon Rhythallt flows out, later becoming the Seiont and emptying into the Menai Strait at Caernarfon. Water activities are not permitted within 200m of the bridge at the northern end, so please give it a wide berth to avoid interfering with the wildlife and plant species.

Heading back along the southern shore you are treated to a view up the Llanberis Pass, one of the finest views in Wales and there is plenty of time to enjoy it. Snowdon rises on the right (west) side of the pass, and Glyder Fawr and Glyder Fach on the left (east) side, providing a truly spectacular panorama.

This shore is also wooded, though not as densely as the north-western side and the road runs close to the lake for several hundred metres but is inaccessible. Below the road, a footpath follows the side of the lake along an old railway track. At the narrowest part of the lake there are a series of small inlets and islands which are great fun to explore, particularly with young children. They will be delighted to discover a secret pirate cove or a Red Indian backwater (your choice).

After this you arrive at Llanberis. There are several slipways and many tourist attractions. These are probably best enjoyed after you have changed out of your paddling kit, but it is nice to break up the journey by stopping to visit a café for a brew and a slice of cake. You could even drop in at 'Pete's Eats' for a pint of tea and one of their famous omelettes.

Heading around to the end of the lake you will find the narrow inflow from Llyn Peris, Padarn's smaller sister. Llyn Peris can be fun to explore but stay away from any outflows from the hydro scheme.

From the river's mouth, it is 100m to the lagoons that you launched from. Navigate your way back inside and head back to the car, another Welsh canoe classic under your belt.

03 Upper River Glaslyn (WW)

 OS Sheet 115 | **Llyn Gwynant to above Aberglaslyn Gorge** | **9km**

Shuttle	6 miles via A498
Start	Roadside A498, Llyn Gwynant, SH 648 519
Finish	Roadside A498, Aberglaslyn Pass, SH 592 469

Introduction

The River Glaslyn is best known among canoeists for the Aberglaslyn Gorge, a short section of grade 4/5 that is fearsome in higher water. The section we have described isn't nearly as difficult although it is not without excitement, and offers some stunning views in a beautiful valley.

The river starts from the Glaslyn (Welsh for 'Blue Lake'), nestled high up, close to the summit of Snowdon. The river plummets, losing over five hundred metres of altitude in the first six kilometres, before entering Llyn Gwynant where our trip starts.

The only settlement on the river is Beddgelert towards the end of the trip. This is a pretty village strung out along the valley of the Colwyn, with a population of about 450.

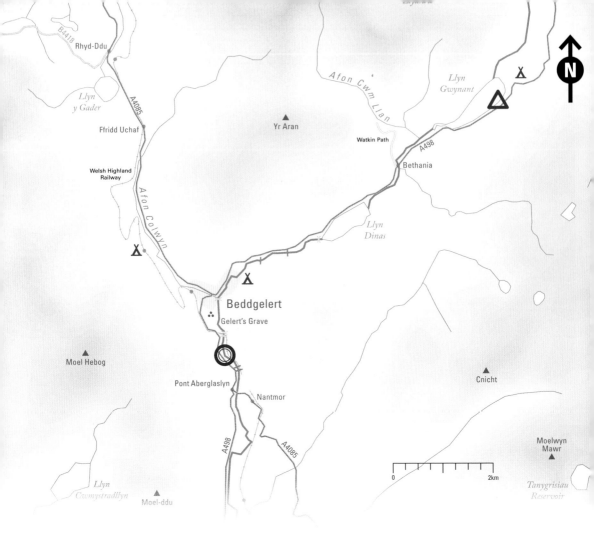

It is most famous for the story (or myth) of the dog Gelert, the adored and faithful hound of Prince Llewelyn the Great. Returning from a hunting trip one day, he found his infant son missing, and the dog covered in blood. Thinking that Gelert had killed the baby, he slew him with his sword, only to find the baby safe, and a wolf killed nearby. Very remorseful, he built a grave and memorial for Gelert, still visible, near the banks of the Glaslyn.

Other settlements nearby include Caernarfon on the Menai Strait, thirteen miles north-west, on the A4085 road, and Porthmadog and Criccieth to the south on the coast. Portmeirion, the fantasy Italianate village created by Clough Williams-Ellis between 1925 and 1975 is accessible from Penrhyndeudraeth, east of Porthmadog. It has served as the location for numerous films and TV shows.

The summit of Snowdon is only three miles to the north, and three of the walking routes up the mountain start nearby; the Pyg and Miners' Tracks from Llanberis Pass, and the Watkin Path, halfway between Llyn Gwynant and Llyn Dinas.

Water level

Information on water levels is available from www.rainchasers.com or www.riverlevels.uk. Enter 'Glaslyn' or 'Beddgelert' in the 'search' box to find the appropriate page.

The river level must be a minimum of 0.75 on the gauge in Beddgelert. Always check the physical level indicators, especially higher up. Around 1.0 on the gauge gives good flows and interesting rapids.

The level indicators are at the following locations:

- Where the river flows out of Llyn Gwynant;
- Where the river passes under the A498 between the lakes;
- Where the river flows out of Llyn Dinas;
- At the egress of this section, before the Aberglaslyn Gorge.

There is a local agreement for this section involving the National Trust and several other local organisations. Snowdonia Active has made available an electronic version of the National Trust's 'Enjoy the River Glaslyn' leaflet with map.

http://www.snowdonia-active.com/upload/documents/Glaslyn_Arrangement_leaflet.pdf

Campsites

Llyn Gwynant Campsite at the head of the lake offers camping and barn accommodation in a beautiful setting. Cae Du Campsite is close to the river in Beddgelert and 'Camping in the Forest' is signposted from the A4085 to Caernarfon.

Access and egress

There are a couple of small lay-bys about halfway along Llyn Gwynant where you can park less than 10m from the water. A small charge (£4 in 2016) for launching applies, payable to Llyn Gwynant Campsite. There are two car parks along the route – offering access or egress if desired – where the river runs under the A498 after Llyn Gwynant (SH 628 506) and at the end of Llyn Dinas (SH 609 492).

It is **essential** that you check the egress above Aberglaslyn Gorge as it is not marked and the grade 4 gorge is immediately downstream.

From the river – immediately after an island, there is a series of eddies on the right-hand side and a path running close to the road (SH 592 469). Egress onto this path.

By road – if travelling up the valley from the south, the A498 from Tremadog closely follows the Glaslyn along its floodplain. The A4085 joins from the east across a bridge at Nantmor. The tumbling Aberglaslyn Gorge is immediately above this bridge. The egress (SH 592 469) is about 0.75km upstream of the bridge/junction.

Description

Launching onto Llyn Gwynant you are treated to views of Y Lliwedd, part of the Snowdon range. The lake feels remote and is normally very quiet, even in the summer months. Opposite the lay-by is a large rock which, with a bit of imagination, looks like an elephant. There are several places to jump in (assuming the water is warm enough).

Head west on the lake until you find the river flowing out. The river is narrow and fast flowing to begin but with no hazards or rapids of note. It winds its way through woodland and before long, a tributary joins on the right; the Afon Cwm Llan which adds to the flow.

The river continues through pleasant farmland and to the right there are magnificent views up the Watkin Path towards Snowdon. After a short while the river passes under the road and follows it for about 1km, before entering Llyn Dinas.

Llyn Dinas is often windy. The road runs along the northern shore and at the western end there is a possible access point. The Glaslyn continues on its way, draining out of the lake under a footbridge. A nice wave can form here at certain levels.

This next section is the highlight of the run with several great grade 2 rapids, some quite long but all straightforward. There are boulder garden type rapids at lower water levels and nice bouncy wavetrains in higher flows. The gradient increases as the river enters the confines of Beddgelert, where the Afon Colwyn joins from the right-hand side.

Easy rapids continue as Beddgelert is gradually left behind and 500m after the edge of the village, the river passes under two narrow bridges in close succession. The egress is 100m further, on the right-hand side, near the main road.

Pontcysyllte Aqueduct, Llangollen canal | Ray Goodwin

North East Wales

North East Wales is dominated by the long River Dee, one of the most famous rivers in Wales for paddlers. The focal point of the Dee Valley is Llangollen, a Mecca for canoeists. The town rose to prominence in the early 1960s when fibreglass kayaks were first developed and made the Dee rapids and falls possible.

This historic town has something to offer everyone, with a wide range of cafés, bars, hotels, restaurants, guesthouses, B&Bs, cottages and campsites. It also has many independent shops to browse and interesting places to discover. Visitors can ride on a steam railway or enjoy peace and quiet gliding along the Llangollen Canal on a horse-drawn boat.

The famous Llangollen International Musical Eisteddfod takes place every year during the second week of July. Singers and dancers from around the world are invited to take part in over twenty high-quality competitions, followed, every evening, by a concert where the best and most colourful competitors share the stage with professional artists. Five thousand singers, dancers and instrumentalists from over fifty countries perform to a total audience of over 50,000 during the six days of the event.

Llangollen is part of a UNESCO World Heritage Site which includes eleven miles of canal from Gledrid to the Horseshoe Falls via the spectacular Pontcysyllte Aqueduct, another canoeing 'must' described in this section. The town was granted Cittaslow status in 2013, an award which recognises communities working for the common good, especially in community activities, the arts, and a slow pace of life.

Bala is a small market town which became known to paddlers in the 1970s, when the National White Water Centre was founded on the reliable dam-released Tryweryn. The river is also popular for rafting, offering the experience of a narrow and exciting rapid river. Llyn Celyn, the supply reservoir, was built between 1960 and 1965, and a village was drowned in the process.

Both the Dee and the Tryweryn have hosted slaloms and whitewater races over the years which have attracted paddlers from all over the UK and across the world.

Autumn on the Lower Dee

04 River Dee (WW)

OS Sheet 117 | Llangollen to Overton Bridge | 26km

Shuttle	10 miles, via A539 from Overton Bridge to Ruabon and Llangollen, 20min
Portages	Possibly two: at Erbistock Weir, SJ 348 414, and Overton Weir, SJ 354 421
Start	Llangollen, downstream of bridge, river left, SJ 217 420
Finish	Overton Bridge, downstream of bridge, river left, SJ 355 428

Introduction

This trip is on a superb section of the beautiful River Dee ('Afon Dyfrdwy' in Welsh). There are plenty of interesting rapids and also some flat water. It is very suitable for open canoe trips, and perfect as a first moving water experience. Take a packed lunch, as you will enjoy a very full day on the river.

The Dee leaves Bala Lake in the east of Gwynedd and, joined by the waters of the Tryweryn, flows one hundred and forty kilometres through the steep-sided valleys of Denbighshire to Connah's Quay on the north coast. The river becomes tidal at Chester. Several tributaries are of whitewater interest, namely the Alwen near Corwen and the Ceiriog near Chirk.

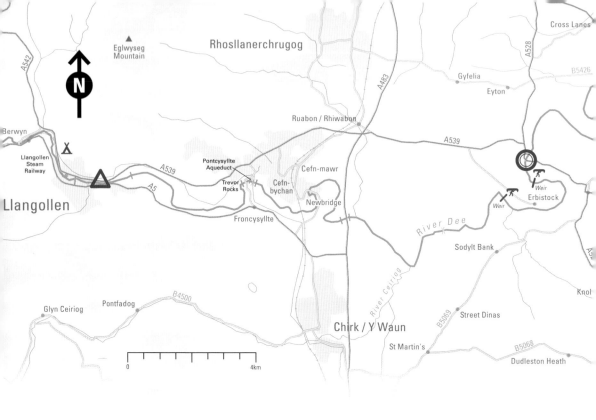

The section described follows a pretty wooded valley down towards the English border. The river is narrow all the way and loses height rapidly. Trevor Rocks Rapid is believed to be the site of the very first canoe slalom held in the UK in 1939. It remained in use until the 1960s. Below Trevor, the river passes under the towering Pontcysyllte Aqueduct. At times, the Dee winds through fairly industrial parts, but this is never obvious from deep down in the wooded valley. After Newbridge, and especially below the high and busy A5 viaduct, the river becomes surprisingly remote, with few visible habitations.

There is a good flow until just before Erbistock, after which the river becomes much slower. There are two weirs on the route; one at Erbistock and the other before the Overton Bridge, not far from the end.

Novices, please note that access isn't easy on the second half of the trip.

Water level

Information on water levels is available from www.rainchasers.com or www.riverlevels.uk. Enter 'Dee' or 'Corwen' in the 'search' box to find the appropriate page. The optimum flow for paddling is 0.55 on the gauge at Corwen, after the Alwen confluence.

A compensation flow provided at the Bala sluices keeps the river at a minimum level. However, it is worth checking that there is enough water to paddle a canoe easily below Llangollen Bridge and at Trevor Rocks Rapid.

Campsites

The Boat Inn, on the river at Erbistock, allows diners to camp. Alternatively, there are several campsites around Llangollen.

Access and egress

Llangollen, downstream of the bridge, river left, via a public car
park behind the Ponsonby Arms – SJ 217 420

Trevor Rocks (river left) – SJ 267 420

Ty Mawr Country Park, river left, after the beach, up the steps before
the viaduct, footpath to the car park, 500m – SJ 277 413

Erbistock, Boat Inn, left bank – SJ 354 414

Overton Bridge, downstream, river left, via a field to the road – SJ 355 428

Parking is possible at the Cross Foxes pub, up the hill on the left. The proprietors are always happy to allow paddlers to leave cars in the rear car park, as long as you promise to have a drink or something to eat afterwards (highly recommended!).

All other bridges are very high and access would be extremely difficult.

Description

The Ponsonby Arms is on the way out of town on the shuttle route. The public car park at the back of the pub gives access to the river. Upstream, there is a fearsome weir below Llangollen Bridge which should be avoided.

The flow is good, and the town is soon left behind. The first rapid, a 300m wavetrain, is also the longest and a nice warm-up. There are often anglers on this stretch, but they are always friendly. The A539 and the Llangollen Canal are often visible high on the left bank, but otherwise nothing disturbs the peace. Between wooded islands, the river proceeds mainly eastwards, and then turns in a long, slow bend to the left. After a very sharp bend left, and then right with rocky shallows, Trevor Rocks Rapid is by a converted mill on the left bank.

Rounding the right-hand bend, the rapid falls over reefs and steps for about 150m. The left side of the river is often dry, and the right-hand route does need to be steered down. It is fairly easy for kayaks and only a little more complicated for open canoes. Be aware of a second shelf-drop directly under the road bridge, as it is often shielded from view until the last minute. Access to, and egress from, the river is possible via a footpath below the bridge, river left.

The Pontcysyllte Aqueduct is an obvious feature overhead. Break out into the eddy underneath the right-hand arch to find a commemorative plaque only visible from the river. Beginning directly under the central arch is a straightforward (but meaty) rapid, which requires care. Then everything slows down.

The Dee wanders in a left-hand bend around Cefn-bychan, and 1km downstream is the Ty Mawr Country Park on the left. There is a sandy beach, ideal for a stop, and it is possible to egress the river using the steps on the left, 150m further downstream.

A high railway viaduct is next, and then the road bridge at Newbridge, on a sharp right-hand bend. The river then appears to leave civilisation, with a long, wooded bend right and then left for 3km, until it passes under the high A5 viaduct. There are fairly frequent straightforward rapids down this stretch, becoming larger and heavier once past the viaduct. Thick woods abound for a further 2km. From here on, there are shooting estates on both sides of the river. At an obvious bend to the left, the riverbed becomes more gravelly and the River Ceiriog joins from the right, a fairly small tributary at summer levels. The Ceiriog is a super grade 3 whitewater river in its higher reaches. Immediately after the Ceiriog is a short narrow section, with some excellent eddies, for practice.

After this, the Dee slows down, and turns north-easterly for the first time, passing the Gronwen and Pen-y-Lan estates, the latter with a private road bridge. After about 4km of flat water, Erbistock Weir is just around a very sharp bend to the right. The village is still invisible at this point. This weir is potentially **dangerous**, with a central block of concrete and a stopper at high water levels. It may be prudent to **portage** along the footpath on the left bank. In low water, the simplest way is to walk down the left-hand face of the weir. Erbistock village is 500m further, on the left bank, with landing possible at the Boat Inn.

A long bend to the left, followed by several small, tight bends and quiet pools, takes you 3km further on, to Overton Weir. This is high and sloping and has **dangerous** metal spikes down its face. Paddling it can be a bit of an **epic** in high water. The weir on the right side down an angled, rocky chute can be shot if there is enough water to cover the rocks. In higher levels it becomes wider and more difficult to stay on line and it would be **dangerous** in very high water. Alternatively, you can **portage** on the right-hand bank before this chute, or on the left side, but this brings you very close to the mill house.

The end is 500m further at Overton Bridge, obvious downstream. Egress on the left side, up through a field.

05 Bala Lake

OS Sheets 125 and OL23 | Round trip of 12km

Start/Finish	Bala, the beach by the leisure centre, SH 921 354
Start/Finish	Llangower, small car park by the railway station, SH 902 321

Introduction

Bala Lake ('Llyn Tegid' in Welsh) is the largest natural body of water in Wales; six kilo-metres long, nearly one kilometre wide, and covering an area of 1200 acres. It came into being when a moraine lip at the Bala end of the lake held back the waters of the River Dee and flooded a small part of the Bala Fault, a geological feature which trends north-east to south-west and extends offshore into Cardigan Bay. This type of lake is known as a glacial ribbon lake.

The lake is home to roach, eel, brown trout and the unique and critically endangered species 'gwyniad' which was trapped in the lake at the end of the last ice age. Its survival is threatened by the 'ruffe', a fish species introduced in the 1980s which eats the eggs and the young of the gwyniad. Some gwyniad eggs have been transferred to another nearby lake in an attempt to prevent extinction.

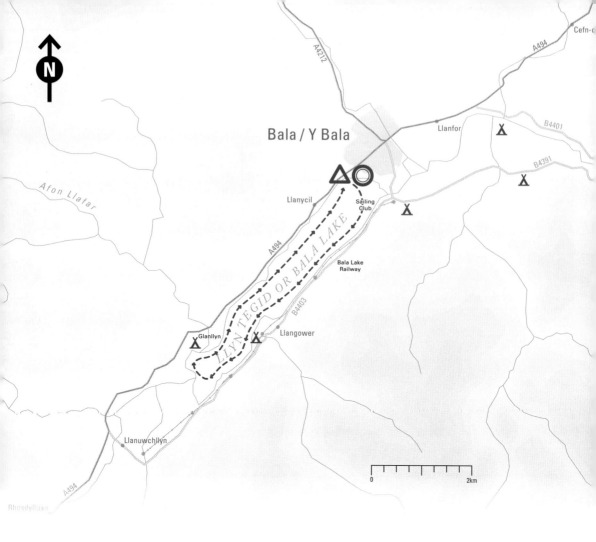

At the north-eastern end of the lake, the town of Bala has several pubs, cafés and restaurants as well as a range of shops for supplies.

There is a small day charge for paddling on the lake which is payable to the warden who may be seen out and about, or at the warden centre on the foreshore. Weekly and annual permits are available if you intend to visit regularly.

Campsites

Glanllyn is on the north shore of the lake at the western end and Pant yr Onnen on the southern shore, near Llangower. Both offer launching facilities.

Access and egress

Bala, the beach by the leisure centre – SH 921 354

Llangower, the small car park by the railway station – SH 902 321

Description

The lake is described in a clockwise direction from the Bala foreshore. Leaving the beach and heading east, the shore is a boggy area of flat, grassy marshland on the outskirts of town. After 1km of paddling the outflow of the River Dee is reached. Depending on the water levels, it may be possible to paddle down a short way to the sluice gates and back. Beware of getting too close to the gates as the water flows underneath them and it could be extremely **dangerous**. The lake water level can fluctuate massively in periods of high rainfall and the fields to the south-west are often underwater.

Heading south-west from the northern end of the lake, Aran Benllyn (885m) dominates the view. The name of this peak translates as 'head of the lake' – appropriate, as you will be able to see it for the duration of your paddle.

Continuing along the shore, you will pass Bala Sailing Club. The town and roads are left behind and there is more of a feeling of being away from it all. A narrow-gauge railway follows the shore and occasionally a steam locomotive will pass by carrying a host of waving tourists. The countryside is a mixture of farm and woodland and there is plenty of opportunity to spot small mammals and birds. The paddle becomes more and more remote until Llangower Point. The beach on the south side of the point is the Llangower access point and makes an ideal lunch spot, sheltered from the wind. You may find 'canoe guru' Ray Goodwin launching here for one of his many training courses or a personal coaching session. Say "hello" and avoid being forced into buying a copy of his wonderful book.

After the point, you enter the south-eastern reaches of the lake and there are lots of small bays and river inlets to explore. At the far end of the lake, many of these bays have interesting grassy mounds that are wonderful for children to investigate. The inflow of the River Dee can be explored upriver, but you may need to pole your canoe.

Continuing clockwise, there is a large bay with Glanllyn, the Welsh-speaking outdoor centre, the venue for the Welsh Open Canoe Symposium, and the Glanllyn campsite, which has hosted the 'Song of the Paddle Big Meet', one of the largest gatherings of open canoes in the UK. This bay is sheltered and is an excellent place for beginners to experience their first solo paddle, or for the more capable to practise rescue or rolling techniques.

Heading north-east out of the bay, the main A494, originally a Roman road, soon comes into view and follows the shore, reassuringly close by, for the remainder of the trip. The road is hidden from view by a narrow band of woodland which dampens the noise quite nicely. In this woodland, there are several nice sneaky bivvy spots where a very small group could enjoy an evening under tarp.

Continuing north, the finish is in sight. The fetch increases and with the prevailing wind from behind, the waves may build. Occasionally, on very blustery days, it is possible to surf right onto the car park – a wonderful end to a paddle.

Bala sluices

The original sluice gates were built by Thomas Telford to help maintain the flow in the Llangollen Canal. The modern sluices partly fulfil the same purpose but also control the amount of water going down the river. In summer the lake is normally kept at 'recreational level' to enable craft to operate closer to the shore. In winter the level is dropped, ready to take the peak off winter floods.

© Tryweryn boulder garden | Ray Goodwin

06 Lower River Tryweryn (WW)

 OS Sheets 125 and OL 18 | Canolfan Tryweryn to Bala | 6.5km

Shuttle	4.5 miles via the A4212, 10min
Portages	Possibly the rapid after the bridge at halfway, and Bala Mill Falls (grade 3+), easily portaged using the specially adapted leat, river right
Start	Canolfan Tryweryn, SH 893 400
Finish	Bala, car park, SH 929 362

Introduction

In the 1960s the Tryweryn Valley was dammed to create a supply of drinking water for the Wirral and parts of Liverpool. The result was Llyn Celyn reservoir from which water is released to form the excellent sections of whitewater below. The Tryweryn is a veritable honeypot for paddlers in the dry summer months. It is also famous for the headquarters of Canoe Wales, Canolfan Tryweryn and as a competition venue for several whitewater disciplines.

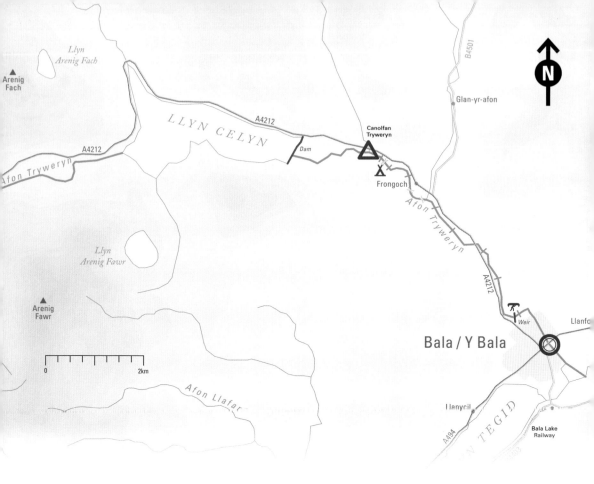

The town of Bala is at the end of the trip, and offers the usual shops, pubs, hotels, a campsite, and the possibility of paddling on Bala Lake (Llyn Tegid).

The Upper Tryweryn, the section from the dam down to where our trip starts, is beyond the scope of this book. It is excellent grade 3 whitewater, possible in an open canoe but requiring a high degree of skill. The section described below is commonly known as the Lower Tryweryn and is a superb river with great scenery, a remote feel and lots of brilliant rapids. You will need to be able to steer well, read the water, and get eddies first time! There is no 'drifting' on this river.

Water level

The Tryweryn is dam released which provides a fairly consistent 9 or 10 cumecs. In periods of heavy rain, however, the many tributaries and ground water can increase the flow to significantly more than this. The route description is with a 'normal' release and little additional flow.

Canolfan Tryweryn (01678 520826) provides a recorded message, regularly updated, detailing upcoming water releases and access issues.

Campsites

Tyn Cornel Camping is just downstream of the start and offers riverside camping in a lovely setting, (01678 520759).

Access and egress

Park in the car park on the left as you enter Canolfan Tryweryn. Cross the small bridge and head downstream until below the steep Chapel Falls.

For the egress, paddle under the A494 road bridge through the archway furthest right and get out in the small square-shaped eddy cut into the bank. It is important not to miss this as there is a dangerous weir 300m downstream.

Description

The rapids start right away with some fast, narrow jets leading down to Campsite Wave, a right-angle turn in the river with a nice wave to play on.

Just after this wave is the small bridge to Tyn Cornel Camping. Downstream, there is a fantastic steep slide of a rapid that narrows to form a wave at the bottom. This rapid defines the run in terms of size; it is as big as it gets and has a pool and slack water below to pick up the pieces from any mishap.

From here, the river has lots of great grade 2 rapids with nice eddies, interspersed with flat sections allowing you to get your breath back. The road comes close on the left, and just after there is a blind left-hand bend. It is best to stop in the eddy on the outside of this bend to **inspect** the line downstream where an island can catch out the unsuspecting. Pass the island river left, as it is normally more fun. This leads into a lovely continuous section with lots of small eddies, a few islands and some rocks to avoid; the best part of the river.

Easier water leads down to the road bridge. You are a little over halfway. The rapid below the bridge runs both sides of an island and the entry moves are quite technical. The author was caught out here, so **inspecting** the line in advance is recommended. This is easily done from the left-hand bank where it is possible to **portage**. Once in the rapid, there is a lovely wavetrain down the centre with eddies on both sides.

The rapids become more spaced out and gentler in the lead-in to Bala Mill Falls. This grade 3+ rapid is easily **portaged** by paddling down a leat that has been adapted to provide a gentle trip through the woods, followed by a short walk down the hill which puts you back in below the falls. The leat is well signposted and the entrance is above a river-wide weir-like slide.

Paddlers who decide to run Bala Mill Falls will run the slide and then enjoy 200m of grade 3, arguably the best section on the river and definitely warranting the grade. Clean eddy lines, nice waves and lots of satisfying moves lead straight into the falls, so keep an eye out downstream. There is a good-sized eddy, river left above the falls, from which a line can be decided. The drop itself is a two-tier shelf with lots of aerated water. A straightforward line down the centre with a bit of speed nearly always yields a successful outcome.

From here, down to the egress, is 700m of grade 1 which makes a lovely venue for poling open canoes and for beginners to get their first taste of moving water.

Enjoy the calm after the storm and float down savouring the excitement of one of Wales' best summer whitewater runs. Get out immediately after the bridge on the right, pop into one of Bala's excellent pubs for a drink, or maybe drive back up for another lap?

07 Llangollen Canal

 OS Sheets 126 and 117 | **St Martin's Moor to Llangollen** | **20km**

Shuttle	10 miles, via A5 and local roads at each end, 25min
Note	There are two tunnels on this trip; Chirk and Whitehouses, both require care and the use of a bright torch. Passage is subject to the terms imposed on canoeists by the Rivers and Canals Trust.
Start	St Martin's Moor, SJ 315 357
Finish	Horseshoe Falls, B5103 bridge over the canal, Llangollen, SJ 198 432

Introduction

The Llangollen Canal is one of the most beautiful and spectacular in the UK. The Pontcysyllte Aqueduct, 307m long and 38m high, spans the Dee Valley and is one of Thomas Telford's crowning glories. In addition to paddling across this amazing structure, at the Horseshoe Falls you will be able to go further than any of the power boats or the small horse-drawn tourist boats as you have the advantage of a shallower draught!

The canal is very popular midsummer, so for a quieter trip, a visit in spring or autumn is recommended. The Llangollen Canal, originally known as the Ellesmere Canal, leaves

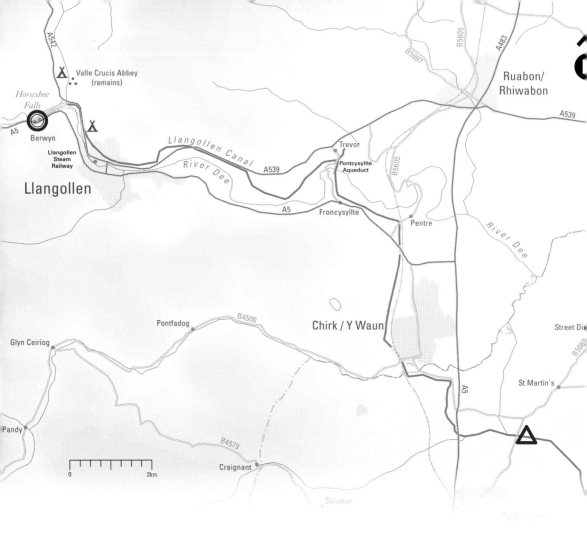

the Shropshire Union at Hurleston Junction near Middlewich. The latter part, near Llangollen, was built as a feeder from the River Dee to provide water to the canals in Shropshire and Cheshire. This is why the Llangollen end survived when, in 1944, much of the Shropshire Union waterway was abandoned.

The three tunnels and two aqueducts required advanced engineering skills and were designed by Thomas Telford. Superintendent Matthew Davidson and William 'Merlin' Hazeldine constructed the massive iron troughs for the aqueducts. Every few years, the water is drained by blocking the ends of the troughs and removing a plug in the middle to let the water trickle out into the Dee!

The canal is unusual in that it has a constant flow from Llantysilio at the western end. Ninety-six million gallons of water pass down it from the Dee every week, a staggering figure.

Llangollen is famous for its cultural International Musical Eisteddfod and as a centre for canoesport.

Water level

The water level is maintained for navigation, but the canal is very shallow near the Horseshoe Falls.

Campsites

There are none near the start, but several around Llangollen. Abbey Farm, next to Valle Crucis Abbey, is a mile from the end of the trip.

Access

St Martin's Moor – SJ 315 357

Rhoswiel Bridge – SJ 297 362

Gledrid Bridge – SJ 298 369

Chirk Bank Bridge – SJ 292 371

Chirk, north end of Chirk Tunnel – SJ 283 378

Pentre – SJ 286 408

Froncysyllte – SJ 271 413

Short Arm (Ruabon Branch and Moorings) – SJ 272 423

Llangollen – SJ 214 422

Horseshoe Falls, B5103 bridge over the canal, Llangollen – SJ 198 432

Description

The start is at St Martin's Moor, a subsidiary village to the larger St Martin's, half a mile away. There is parking and a wharf. The canal heads west, through fairly flat countryside and under frequent small road bridges. The surroundings then become more built-up. The canal winds its way around the east of Weston Rhyn village, passes under the main A5 road and turns north, then west around the town of Chirk.

The aqueduct over the River Ceiriog, 216m long and 21m high, gives the first of the great views on this trip. You can peer over to glimpse the whitewater section upstream. Chirk Tunnel (420m long) follows almost immediately. Take care in the tunnels and always keep watch for powerboats. The tunnels have a towpath with a protective railing and canoes could be lined through if you were nervous.

A straight stretch follows, with the railway on the right bank. A left turn in the canal opens up the vista of the Dee Valley, a great sight, and of the aqueduct ahead. The village of Froncysyllte, or 'Fron' is on the left side, and suddenly you are on the Pontcysyllte Aqueduct. Be warned that there will be little between you and the drop on one side of the iron trough (the other side has the tow path)! It is, however, a fabulous feeling, looking down onto the River Dee and its rapids. The rapid upstream is Trevor Rocks, where slalom competitions used to take place regularly in the 1950s and 60s. It is said that this was the first slalom site in Wales.

Once on the other side, the canal widens. This was previously a branch that headed north-east to Ruabon and Chester, but now it is just a marina and tourist attraction.

The canal turns left, and Trevor village is below. The site of a former chemical works, once the mainstay of local employment, is away to the right.

The route winds along the north side of the Dee Valley and all is green and lush. The canal parallels the main road and then passes under it about one mile before Llangollen.

Llangollen is a small compact town with many cafés and pubs, and the canal is just above the street on the north side of the Dee. You could park your canoe and wander around the town. The best place to leave it would be on the bank by the road bridge. The railway station has been restored and trains run for a short distance. At the heart of the town is the bridge over the Dee, where locals and tourists gather to watch the falls above the bridge.

The canal is now narrow and shallow, but fine for canoes. It is a mere two miles of very pleasant paddling up to Llantysilio, and a few hundred yards further to the ultimate objective, the pretty Horseshoe Falls. The canal ends at the Horseshoe Falls, but egress is about 50m back up the canal where the B5103 crosses overhead. There is a car park with toilet block above the canal at SJ 197 432.

Horseshoe Falls

The falls are a beautifully simple solution to the problem of supplying water to the canal. They were designed by Telford and are in fact a weir. It measures a metre high, and is the width of the river. It backs up the water and feeds it off at the side, into the canal.

Lake Vyrnwy dam

East Wales

This area is made up predominantly of Powys, the long, thin county on the east side of Wales along the border with England. It is the largest county in area, but the least populated. It is almost totally hilly, making the north to south road very slow.

Although less well-known to visitors than the mountains of Snowdonia, or the beaches of Pembrokeshire, it has plenty to offer in addition to peacefulness. Offa's Dyke, the ancient border fortification to keep the Welsh out of Mercia, built in the 8th century, is one of the loneliest and most interesting long-distance walks in the UK. One hundred and seventy-seven miles from Prestatyn on the north coast, to near Chepstow in the south on the tidal Wye, it often takes two weeks to complete. There are tough sections in the Shropshire Hills and the Brecon Beacons, and the whole walk has 28,000 feet of ascent, the same as Everest!

The main towns in Powys are Newtown and Welshpool in the Severn Valley, Brecon, and Ystradgynlais, just outside Swansea in the Tawe Valley. Brecon is worth visiting, as is the tiny and picturesque Montgomery.

The area includes the upper reaches of two of the longest and most important rivers in the UK, namely the Severn and the Wye. They rise close together on Plynlimon in Mid Wales, but flow in vastly different directions – the Severn, north-east to Shrewsbury, the Wye, south to Builth Wells and Hereford. Eventually they join at the Severn Estuary.

Powys also includes several spectacular reservoirs and dams; the Elan Valley complex west of the Wye, the lonely and isolated Lake Vyrnwy, Llyn Brianne at the head of the Tywi, and the Clywedog Reservoir, a tributary of the Severn.

Castles abound along the border and there are numerous ruins between Builth Wells and New Radnor. Brecon and Sennybridge both have castles, Powis Castle near Welshpool is well-known and Montgomery Castle, overlooking the Welsh border and the Severn Valley, is a 'not-to-miss' site, with a truly spectacular view of the surrounding countryside.

There is walking, cycling and horse riding galore as well as many small towns and villages to visit.

Montgomery town from the castle

© Penarth Weir, River Severn, Newtown

08 Upper River Severn

OS Sheets 136 and 126 | Caersws to just before Welshpool | 49km

Shuttle	17 miles, via the A483 and A489, 35min
Portages	One definite at Penarth Weir, below Newtown, SO 139 926. Possibly, in high water, the weir at the A490 bridge near Welshpool, SJ 228 041
Start	Caersws, SO 032 916
Finish	A483 lay-by, north of Welshpool, SJ 248 100

Introduction

The Upper River Severn is a two-day trip. It is an easy river with nearly always enough water, fairly good access, and plenty of sights. It is possible to shorten the journey to one day by starting at Abermule.

The main road running through the Upper Severn Valley has been improved in recent years, and is very fast. It links the Midlands, via Shrewsbury, to Aberystwyth and the beaches of Mid Wales.

The Severn drops from the flanks of Plynlimon, in a brief whitewater stretch, to Llanidloes and a flatter valley. The start of the trip described is a little further downstream where there is a bit more water.

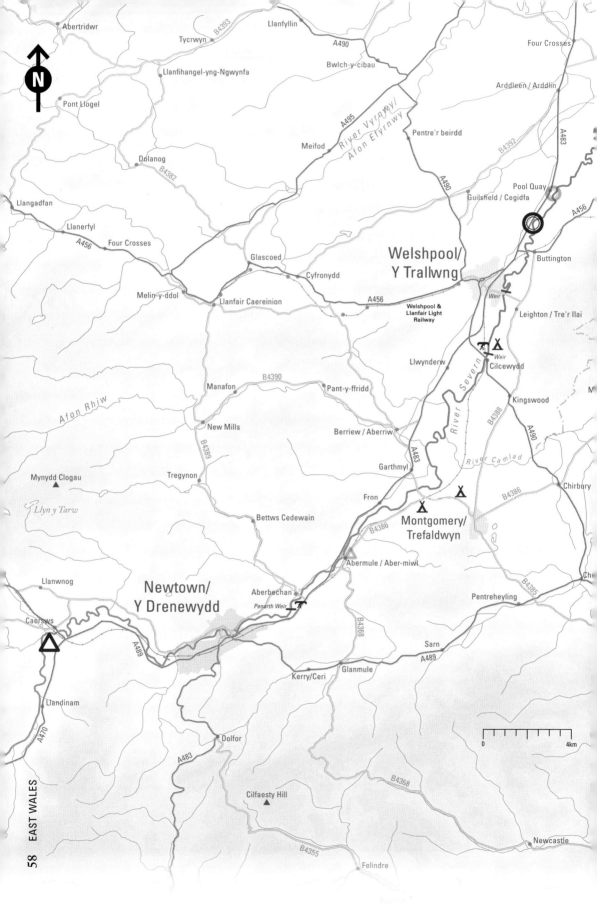

N

Abertridwr
Tycrwyn
Llanfyllin
Four Crosses
A4393
Llanfihangel-yng-Ngwynfa
A490
Bwlch-y-cibau
Arddleen / Arddlin
Pont Llogel
A495
River Vyrnwy / Afon Efyrnwy
Pentre'r beirdd
B4392
A483
Meifod
Dolanog
A490
Pool Quay
B4382
Guilsfield / Cegidfa
A456
Llangadfan
Llanerfyl
A456
Four Crosses
Welshpool/
Y Trallwng
Buttington
Glascoed
Weir
Leighton / Tre'r llai
Cyfronydd
A456
Melin-y-ddol
Welshpool &
Llanfair Caereinion
Llanfair Light
Railway
Weir
Cilcewydd
Afon Rhiw
B4390
Llwynderw
River Severn
Manafon
Pant-y-ffridd
Kingswood
A490
B4389
New Mills
Berriew / Aberriw
B4388
Mynydd Clogau
Tregynon
Garthmyl
River Camlad
Chirbury
A483
Llyn y Tarw
Bettws Cedewain
Fron
B4386
Montgomery/
Trefaldwyn
B4386
Llanwnog
Abermule / Aber-miwl
Pentreheyling
Newtown/
Y Drenewydd
Aberbechan
B4385
Ch
Caersws
Penarth Weir
B4368
A489
Sarn
Pentreheyling
Kerry/Ceri
Glanmule
A489
Llandinam
A470
Dolfor
A483
0   4km
Cilfaesty Hill
B4368
B4355
Newcastle
Felindre

The section down to Newtown winds through low green pastures and marshland. The loops in the river are impressive and may, from time to time, form oxbow lakes. These are crescent-shaped lakes (often temporary) that form when a meander of a river is cut off from the main channel.

The river flows through the centre of Newtown, but bypasses Welshpool, which can be very busy, especially on market days or bank holidays. The valley gradually widens and by the time you reach the egress point near the English border, the views have opened up over the North Shropshire Plain, with occasional steep little hills suddenly rising above the flat land.

The Montgomery Canal, or what is currently left of it, runs parallel to the north of the river, from downstream of Newtown to below Welshpool. There are plans afoot to restore it and in future years it could become useful for a return journey.

Montgomery

Montgomery is a delightful, planned Georgian town which lies four miles east of the River Severn. The castle sits high above atop a lofty hill in a spectacular position visible from miles around. A drive up the hill, followed by a short walk through a farmyard, will bring you to a truly stupendous view (in good weather) of the whole Upper Severn Valley and the English border. Wales has the most castles per square mile of any of the countries in the UK and this is one of the best!

Water level

The Severn usually has enough water to be paddled, albeit with the odd scrape down a gravel rapid. Information about water levels is available from www.rainchasers.com or https://flood-warning-information.service.gov.uk, select 'Newtown station'. A level of between 0.5m and 1.00m is the most suitable.

Campsites

There are two sites on the east side of the river between Montgomery and Berriew, and other sites to the east of Montgomery, a more touristy area.

Access and egress

This trip starts at Caersws Football Club. Travelling from Newtown on the A489, take the road to the left before the river crossing. Parking is just before the railway bridge, with a short walk to the river.

Caersws – SO 032 916

Newtown (second road bridge) – SO 112 915

Canal bridge at Aberbechan – SO 143 933. To avoid the dangerous Penarth Weir or its long portage, it is possible to launch on the canal at the canal bridge at Aberbechan and paddle a short distance until the canal is alongside the river. Please note that there is very little space for vehicle parking.

Abermule Bridge – SO 162 951

Buttington Bridge – SJ 246 089

A483 lay-by north of Welshpool – SJ 248 100

The Montgomery Canal

The Montgomery Canal leaves the Llangollen Canal at Frankton Junction and used to run 35 miles to Newtown. The countryside is beautiful and unspoilt, and wildlife is plentiful. As has often occurred in history, competition from the railway made the canal uneconomic and it was abandoned in 1944. Nowadays, the canal is navigable from the Shropshire Union/Llangollen Canal at Frankton, for seven miles to Gronwyn Wharf, near Maesbury Marsh. The next eight miles or so are dry or unnavigable. From Arddlin, however, the canal is open through to Welshpool, where there is a lovely, but busy, canal basin with moorings. The navigable section ends just past Berriew. Beyond Garthmyl, the bed of the canal becomes a well signposted long-distance footpath. In Newtown, remnants of the canal are still visible, and a canal preservation society hopes to restore it someday. The tow path between Welshpool and Newtown is popular for walking and cycling in peaceful countryside.

Description

The first stretch out of Caersws is strewn with litter and sometimes even supermarket trolleys, but buildings are soon left behind. The main road is always on the right bank, and the railway crosses the river twice. Newtown comes into view. There is a grade 2 rapid on the approach to the town, and another below the second road bridge. Access is possible just downstream of the second bridge.

The **dangerous** Penarth Weir is 3km after leaving Newtown, hidden around a leafy corner. It has a double drop; the first sheer drop is onto flat concrete, followed by the second, a slide which finishes in a stopper. Land and **portage** on the left bank. This entails a long walk behind a chain-link fence to access the river downstream after the weir. The right bank has a steep cliff, which would make a portage very difficult. The channel leading off the left side of the weir is the original top-up system for the Montgomery Canal.

Canal and river now run in parallel. It is 2km to the A483 bridge and then the Abermule Bridge, where there is parking on the road verge, used by anglers visiting the canal.

After 1km, the canal goes off to the north (left), as the valley widens. The railway and the B4386 are now on the right bank. At the B4385 bridge over the river, the town of Montgomery is two miles to the right.

The river meanders more, and the River Camlad (sometimes paddled) joins from the right. The next road bridge is the A490 from Ludlow to Welshpool. There is a weir ahead and care must be taken. It is worth **inspecting** before paddling. In high water, consider **portaging**, but in low to medium water the steps on either side can be shot.

The river is now approaching Welshpool, though it does not flow through the town. Downstream of the minor road bridge there is a sloping weir which does not usually present any problem. It is a further winding 3km to Buttington Bridge, a possible egress point, but with practically no parking.

The recommended egress is 1km further on, where the river is alongside the A483. A lay-by has been built, with easy steps down to the river, though these can still be a challenge with a loaded boat.

Variation

It is possible to paddle 2km further to Pool Quay. However, the track to the road is rather muddy and the lay-by offers little protection from the very fast traffic thundering along the dead straight A483. It would be best to inspect before committing.

Pool Quay

In far-off days, a quay was built between the River Severn and the new canal to enable goods coming up the river on barges to be transferred, at the river's highest navigable point, onto the canal for onward delivery. The process was repeated for goods travelling the other way. Roads were far less important in those days!

River Banwy | Ray Goodwin

09 River Banwy (WW)

OS Sheet 125 | Llanerfyl to Meifod | 22km

Shuttle	10 miles via A458 & A459, 20min
Portages	Possibly one at the weir, SJ 092 072
Start	Llanerfyl, SJ 031 097
Finish	Meifod, Broniarth Bridge, SJ 156 129

Introduction

This area is just how I imagined Wales; small villages and farmland criss-crossed by small winding roads and streams. Just inside the Welsh border, the River Banwy is easily accessible from the Midlands or the North West.

The Banwy is a relatively short river with two major tributaries; the Twrch and the Gam. It flows into the Vyrnwy (a dam-fed river with classic gorge sections of grade 3) which feeds into the Severn.

This section offers fantastic easy whitewater through rolling farmland and small Welsh villages. Stone bridges, churches and sheep are in abundance and sightings of large birds of prey and otters are not uncommon.

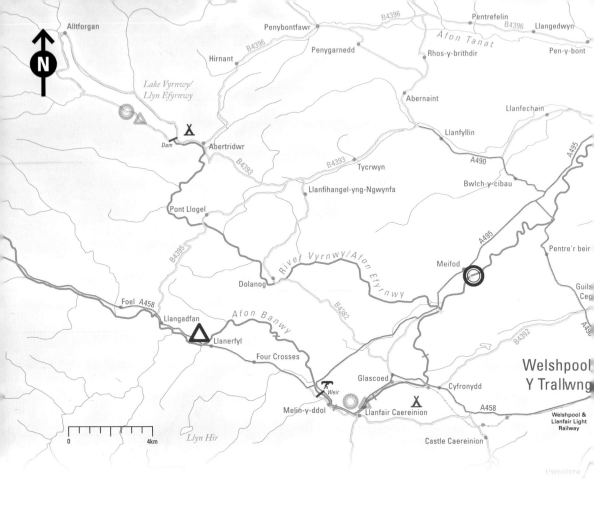

The Welshpool & Llanfair Light Railway runs alongside the river in places. The line opened in 1903 and a train journey is another way to experience this tranquil part of Wales.

Water level

The water level in the Banwy can remain high for up to a week after heavy rain. Information about water levels on this section is available from www.rainchasers.com or www.riverlevels.uk. Enter 'Llanerfyl' in the 'search' box to find the appropriate page. The gauge for Llanerfyl should read at least 1.3.

Campsites

There are none on the river. Strawberry Skys Yurts is 2.5 miles out of Llanfair Caereinion.

Access and egress

At Llanerfyl, head west out of the village, cross the river and turn immediately right. Park here, as the road is wide (SJ 031 097). Access the river through the gate by the bridge.

Good level on the Banwy | Ray Goodwin

Llanfair Caereinion is at the halfway point – follow signs for 'Steam Railway' down a side road in the village which leads to a large gravel car park on the right, next to the river (SJ 107 068).

At Meifod, take the road signposted 'Rugby Club' out of the village to Broniarth Bridge. Park in the rugby club car park (SJ 156 129) or across the bridge where there is room for one or two cars in a lay-by. Take out upstream of the bridge (there are public footpaths on both sides of the river). River left, up the steps to the measuring station or river right, through a field and over a stile to the road. It is a short walk to the rugby club, which is on the left side of the river.

Description

At Llanerfyl, launch from a stony beach almost directly under the road. The bridge stanchion provides two flows and a central ribbon eddy; ideal for warming up or as a place to entertain oneself while waiting for the shuttle.

The trip starts with nice, easy shingle rapids meandering gently through the quiet countryside. There are plenty of small waves and some nice eddies, as well as the fantastic scenery, to keep you entertained.

After 5km the gradient increases slightly, the banks and trees close in, and the river narrows and quickens its pace. A fantastic section for eddy-hopping follows for approximately 2km. Beware on sharp bends because fallen trees can sometimes be a problem. The river exits this mini-gorge and flows for another 2km before the road bridge and then some islands signal the approach of the **weir**. In low to medium flows, it can be run far right, avoiding the rock shelf that forms the weir. In high flows a powerful **retentive stopper** forms with runnable lines both far left and far right. **Inspection** is highly recommended, and **portage** is straightforward across the field, river left. A huge tree stump provides an excellent platform for photographing those who choose to run the weir.

The best rapids of the trip come immediately afterwards. A series of islands provides a choice of channels and great eddies continue almost all the way into Llanfair Caereinion. The church tower is the first sign of the village then, very quickly, you are under the bridge in the centre and heading back out.

To egress here, take out river left, downstream of the arched footbridge after the village. The car park is 10m from the river bank.

The Welshpool & Llanfair Light Railway follows on the left bank for 2km. The river drops through more shingle rapids and some small, rocky chutes. The road and the railway are soon left behind and after passing a caravan site, the river takes on a wilder feel with steeper, wooded sides and some fantastic longer rapids. These include a natural weir with a long lead-in. It is best to keep right, especially in lower water. This is the section where wildlife sightings are likely, so keep an eye out for kingfishers, buzzards and even mink.

All of a sudden the river flattens out and, as you pass under a triple-arched bridge, you emerge onto the River Vyrnwy. The combined waters of both watercourses create a much wider, more sedate river that meanders through a beautiful green valley. This section is prone to bursting its banks in flood and the course of the river has changed significantly over the years, so take care in high water.

After a few gentle kilometres of the river twisting through farmland, the Broniarth green girder bridge is reached. Egress upstream of the bridge, river right, onto a flat field, or river left, up the steps to the measuring station. In springtime, you will be entertained by lively lambs while waiting for the shuttle vehicle.

Lake Vyrnwy

In the forests to the north of the Banwy lies the large Lake Vyrnwy reservoir. It was created by building a massive stone dam in 1880, for the purpose of supplying Liverpool with water. The six kilometre-long lake and surrounding land is managed by the RSPB and Severn Trent Water. Among the Welsh mountain reservoirs, Vyrnwy looks more like a Canadian wilderness lake than any other, and the conifers add to the attraction. Bird life is plentiful and ospreys are often seen.

There is free car parking around the lake, and boating by concession, supplied by a friendly canoe hire company, situated near the dam and visitor centre. 'Guest boats' are allowed for a small fee.

Erwood Rapids

10 Upper River Wye (WW)

 OS Sheets147 and 161 | **Builth Wells to Llyswen** | **20km**

Shuttle	11 miles, via the A470, which follows the river up the valley, 20min
Start	Builth Wells, SO 040 512
Finish	Llyswen, SO 131 386

Introduction

The Wye ('Afon Gwy' in Welsh) is a major British river rising high up on the southern slopes of Plynlimon Fawr in Mid Wales. It flows south through Rhayader and Builth Wells, before turning east near the English border, to head, via Hereford, to the Severn Estuary at Chepstow – a total of one hundred and sixty kilometres of fairly easy water for the touring paddler.

The Welsh stretch provides great whitewater, and is a well-known classic. In addition, there are several tributaries joining in the Newbridge/Builth Wells area, such as the Eithon, the Irfon and the Elan which provide wonderful paddling when there is water.

UPPER RIVER WYE (WW)

EAST WALES

67

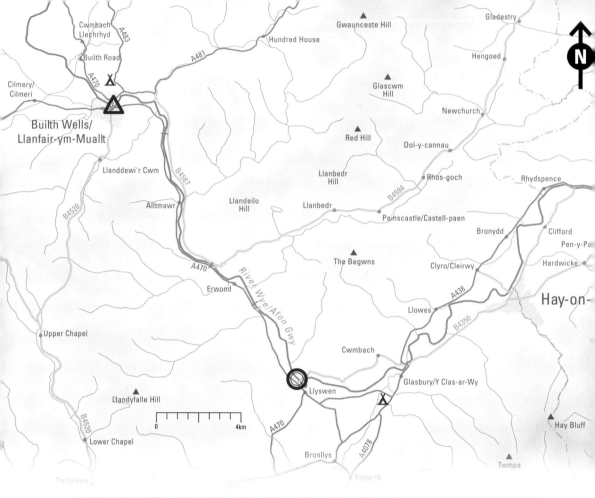

Builth Wells

Builth Wells ('Llanfair-ym-Muallt' in Welsh) was built at the crossing of the River Wye. It remains an important market and road centre for this part of Powys, and still retains many small independent shops.

One version of the origin of the word 'Builth' is that it came from 'Buellt' in Welsh, which could be translated as 'the wild ox of the wooded slope'.

It was a sizeable town by 1277, but suffered several dramas during its history. The Black Death hit in the 1350s and the town was isolated to prevent the spread of the plague. Folk from the countryside would leave food on the banks of a brook for the townspeople who, in return, would throw in money as payment. The brook became known as 'Nant-yr-Arian' or the 'Money Brook', and the name remains in use today.

Several centuries later, around 1690, a great fire laid waste to forty houses.

Every year, during the third week in July, the town is gridlocked while it hosts the Royal Welsh Agricultural Show, a very popular event with the farming community which attracts visitors from all over Wales.

Builth Bridge, River Wye

This middle part of the Wye is testing for open canoeists; low water can be tedious, with much wading in a dry summer, whereas high winter water can provide dangerous conditions. Even though the main road runs parallel to the river all of the way down, there is very little parking, and portages can be very difficult to impossible. In medium water, the rapids aren't too difficult, and it is possible to portage over rocks at the side of the river.

If you enjoy this section, you may be interested in the *River Wye Canoe and Kayak Guide* by Mark Rainsley (Pesda Press, 2016).

Water level

When inspecting the river, the rapids should have a clear passage down them. If all the rocks are covered, the river is high.

Information about water levels on this section is available from www.rainchasers.com or https://flood-warning-information.service.gov.uk. The station for Builth Wells should measure between 1.2m and 2m for an appropriate level.

Campsites

There are campsites at Three Cocks, Bronllys near Talgarth, Builth Wells, and Newbridge-on-Wye. All campsites in the area are fully booked during the third week in July (Royal Welsh Show week).

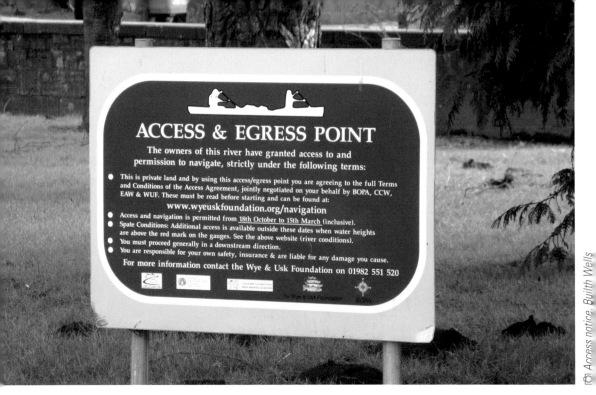

Access and egress

Start at Builth Wells, from the public (paying) car park upriver of the bridge, SO 040 512. Finish at Llyswen, by the bridge, river left, in the signed car park, SO 131 386.

There are no other access/egress points as there is virtually no car parking alongside the river. The road is very busy and fast, and dangerous for portaging. Make sure that you are equipped to paddle the whole stretch.

The Wye and Usk Foundation controls access to the river and has provided designated access points. Please read the following website information:
http://www.wyeuskfoundation.org/navigation/index.php

Webcams can be found here: http://www.wyeuskfoundation.org/conditions/index.php

Description

For most of this section, the Wye runs through a steep-sided wooded valley. The three sets of rapids on this trip are classic bedrock reefs, which all have the same characteristics. They start with a low drop, and finish at the end of a kilometre or so with a final steeper drop, always on the right side of the river. In higher water, this means continuous heavy waves, which can be daunting for those unused to this kind of paddling.

Leaving Builth Wells, the river is wide and slow-moving. For 3km, it runs around several large bends before approaching an obvious steep slope on the left as the hills close in on both sides. The river bends first left, and then right. This is the start of the Llanfaredd Rapids which are about 1km long, and along this section you will pass strange wooded islands, some tiny. There are many rocks in low water, but in high water the islands are covered and only the trees remain visible.

At the finish, the main drop is near the right-hand bank. The A470 road is obvious on the bank. It follows the river all the way down this next stretch. The smaller B4567 road is almost invisible on the left bank.

The sides steepen, with rock faces in places. You will run small rapids, and then Aberedw Castle appears to the left (8km). The small River Edw enters from the left and is followed by cliffs on the left side. After several bends, the Erwood Rapids commence, another 1km of lovely bouncy water, which finishes under the narrow Erwood Bridge. The village is downstream on the right bank.

The river then takes a fairly sharp bend to the left at the village, followed by a right turn and the Llanstephan Rapids are ahead. These are just upstream of the chain bridge at Llanstephan.

This third set of rapids is the most testing, with continuous slabs and drops, becoming steeper near the end. The line is hard down the right-hand side, through the infamous 'Hell Hole' (a large hole). In high water, the stopper across the rest of the river (centre to left) is large and nasty (maybe grade 4). Smaller rapids follow, then about 2.5km further down, there is a surprising final steep drop.

By now, the Llyswen to Boughrood Bridge is in sight, and egress is river left, below the bridge, up a steep muddy bank to a gate. Parking is in Boughrood, and should be signed. Check before paddling, as the parking has changed locations in the past few years. Please ensure that you don't park in the wrong place, and annoy local residents.

Mawddach Estuary | Ray Goodwin

The West Coast

The seventy-five miles long west coast of Wales from Harlech, in Gwynedd to New Quay in Ceredigion (Cardiganshire), provides vast sandy beaches, interesting estuaries and many short rivers that fall rapidly to the sea. The upper reaches are usually hard whitewater, but the last few miles provide an easier experience.

There is no shortage of attractions: Harlech's imposing castle, the golden beaches from Llanbedr down to Barmouth, the Mawddach Estuary, Tywyn Sands, the Dyfi Estuary, the university town of Aberystwyth, with the National Library of Wales, and Cardigan Bay and its coastal resorts. The coastline is well provided with campsites, many in scenic positions. The Wales Coast Path covers a total of 1400km, and a railway line follows the coast for much of the way.

The Snowdonia National Park runs as far south as the Dyfi Estuary. Inland, imposing hills start a short distance back from the sea. Although smaller than the Snowdon range, they are wild, uninhabited, and provide very rough walking. There are some spectacular river gorges above Dolgellau, Machynlleth, and Aberystwyth. The Rheidol Gorge, above Aberystwyth, is especially well-known, with great views at Devil's Bridge, and the upper reaches of the Rheidol are an experimental release area for beavers.

Wildlife abounds. Mid Wales is a UK centre for red kites, and visitors can watch them every day. Dolphins and porpoises often visit the coastal waters, basking sharks are reappearing, and seal pups are evident in the autumn. The RSPB Reserve at Ynys Hir, on the Dyfi Estuary, is famous for its varied bird and mammal life.

The Penmaenpool Toll Bridge

Sunny day on the Mawddach

11 Mawddach Estuary

🐚 **OS Sheet 124** | **Llanelltyd to Fairbourne** | **14km**

Shuttle	10 miles via A470 & A493
Start/Finish	Old Bridge, Llanelltyd, SH 718 193
Start/Finish	Porth Penrhyn Ferry Landing, Fairbourne, SH 617 150

Introduction

This is the most scenic estuary in Wales, overlooked by Cadair Idris from the south and surrounded by stunning wooded hills. The trip can be done in either direction; subject to the tide and the prevailing wind which usually blows off the sea. For this reason, it will generally be easier starting at the seaward end. However, paddling against the sea breeze can make finishing at the seaside that bit more rewarding. Subject to tides and daylight, on a good day, you could paddle there and back again.

Dolgellau is near the start point, and has cafés, restaurants and B&Bs. Barmouth, opposite Fairbourne at the end of the trip, is a typical seaside town; busy in summer, and deserted in winter. It is the starting point for the annual 'Three Peaks Yacht Race', held in early summer. Sailing boats compete, with small crews, and carry runners to tackle

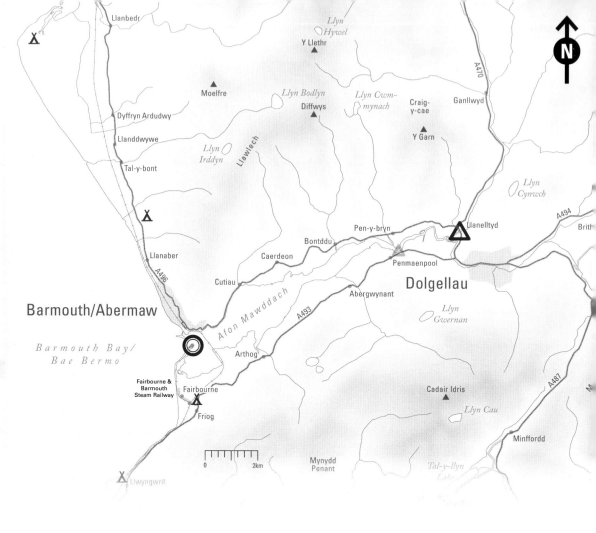

the highest peaks in Wales, England and Scotland. The yachts sail to Caernarfon for Snowdon, Whitehaven for Scafell Pike, and Fort William for Ben Nevis. The record time, so far, is under three days!

Water level

It is necessary to harness the tide, whichever direction you choose to paddle in, so it's worth noting that neap tides barely reach as far as Penmaenpool and that only spring tides make it all the way to Llanelltyd. For an upriver journey you may need to use the alternate finish point. Even when the river is low it is possible to paddle up to Penmaenpool, although there are a few small shingle rapids to negotiate.

At low tide the estuary empties almost completely leaving just a narrow navigable channel. For this reason it is recommended to complete the trip in the highest part of the tide.

High water at Barmouth is Milford Haven HW +0210, low water at Barmouth is Milford Haven LW +0315. If using a Dover tide table, high water at Barmouth is Dover HW -0305.

© Winter paddle on the Mawddach | Ray Goodwin

Campsites

Ynys Faig Camping and Caravan Site is near Fairbourne and there are many sites north of Barmouth, and to the south, nearer to Tywyn.

Kings Youth Hostel (YHA), one of the oldest and most attractive in Wales, is high above, on the south side of the estuary.

Access and egress

Start (or finish) at Old Bridge, Llanelltyd – SH 718 193

Finish (or start) at Porth Penrhyn ferry landing, Fairbourne – SH 617 150

The alternative start/finish is at Penmaenpool Toll Bridge – SH 694 185

Description

Starting from the old bridge at Llanelltyd, the river is shallow with some simple shingle beds to negotiate. There are views of Cadair Idris to the south. The river meanders through fields and it isn't long before it becomes visibly tidal. The muddy banks rise either side and the River Wnion joins from the left. Between here and Penmaenpool is one of Wales' largest areas of reedbeds, home to wild otters and rare wetland bird species such as the red-breasted merganser, redshank and water rail.

At a couple of islands keep left to stay in deep water. You will quickly find yourself entering the estuary. The black and white bridge announces Penmaenpool, the alternative start/finish, with a car park on your left.

From here the river is tidal. At the top of the tide, you can paddle where you please, but if it is low, you will be restricted to a narrow channel all the way to Fairbourne.

The surrounding rolling hills covered in woodland make a truly beautiful setting, particularly on a summer's day. Despite the proximity of roads on both shores, the estuary has a very wild feel to it. The deep channel wanders over to the north shore as you progress towards the sea, and there are some nice secluded beaches surrounded by rocky outcrops.

The channel then heads over to the southern shore and takes you past Ynys Faig Camping and Caravan Site and beyond a rocky hillock into a small cove with some buildings at the water's edge. Just past here, there is a long sandy beach.

Fast approaching is the imposing Barmouth Bridge ('Pont Abermaw' in Welsh), which carries the Cambrian Coast Railway across the estuary. The channel will convey you to the northern end of the bridge where the gaps between stanchions are the widest. It is recommended to pass under here, to avoid hitting the bridge. During a spring tide the current can be fast under the bridge and care must be taken. Beyond, Barmouth is on your right and it is possible to land here. There is an excellent selection of pubs and restaurants in addition to all of the attractions associated with a seaside town. We recommend the excellent ice cream parlour overlooking the harbour.

Fairbourne is opposite Barmouth. Land on the inside of the spit and it is a short walk up to the car park. In low water this walk will be a little further but the sand is firm. Fairbourne has a charm of its own and even a short section of steam railway.

12 River Dysynni

 **OS Sheets 124 and 135 | Abergynolwyn to Pont Dysynni | 12km**

Shuttle	5 miles, via the B4405, 10min
Start	Abergynolwyn, SH 682 072
Finish	Pont Dysynni (the old bridge), SH 598 038

Introduction

This is a lovely little river, flowing from the impressive mountains between the Mawddach and Dyfi estuaries. The bulk of Craig yr Aderyn (Birds' Rock) rises 250 metres from the flat valley floor, adding to the character of the area. Although seeming isolated, this valley is near Barmouth and Dolgellau to the north, and Aberdyfi and Machynlleth to the south, with Tywyn, a well-known Mid Wales holiday resort, at its mouth.

Tywyn, in the far south of the Snowdonia National Park, was at one time known mainly for its caravan sites, but today it offers all types of accommodation. It has a vast sandy beach, and views north-west towards the Lleyn Peninsula and Bardsey Island. It is on the Wales Coast Path, and has a railway station with regular services.

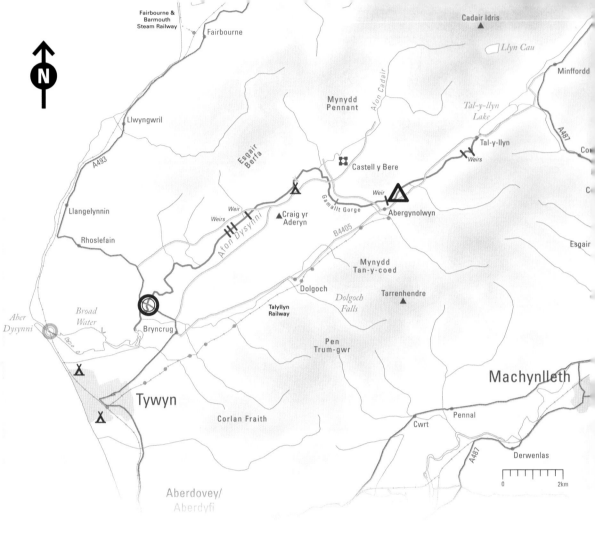

Whereas many west coast rivers drop very quickly down to the sea, and are sustained whitewater, the Dysynni has a reasonable distance of easy water to paddle, including a gorge that looks impressive, but has few difficulties.

The description gives an optional extra of paddling the tidal stretch to the sea, a distance of a further 4.5 kilometres.

The river is not suitable for large groups as it is small, as are the roads in the valley, and parking is very difficult to find.

Water level

The river needs all rocks to be covered.

Campsites

There are plenty of campsites at nearby Tywyn.

River Dysynni valley

The Talyllyn Railway

The Talyllyn Railway runs 11.5km alongside the B4405, very nearly to Abergynolwyn, in a valley parallel to the river. It is an historic narrow-gauge railway which opened in 1866 to carry slate from mines at the head of the valley down to Tywyn. It was an unusual venture for a Welsh railway in that as well as its industrial role, it carried passengers and freight from its opening. Nowadays, tourists flock to ride the train via eight stations, past the Dolgoch Falls, to the forest walks at Nant Gwernol. The railway has popular 'hop-on-and-off' tickets, and is famous for the friendliness of its staff. Abergynolwyn was built to accommodate the slate workers, and is a surprisingly large village for its isolated position.

Access and egress

Abergynolwyn – SH 682 072

Pont Ystumanner – SH 659 078

Pont-y-garth – SH 635 070

Pont Dysynni (old bridge) – SH 598 038

The two middle bridges have very few opportunities for parking, whereas there is space for parking by the old bridge at Pont Dysynni.

Description

First inspect the Gamallt Gorge below the village – this is a super place with trees and rock ledges covered in higher water, and a fairly constant grade 2. In very high water it is a serious proposition due to the risk of hitting trees.

Abergynolwyn is a pretty and friendly village, but access onto the river is awkward. Drive north out of the village to where the river comes close to the road. There is a cemetery on the right side. Park with care, maybe on the grass verge. Access (ask for permission if anyone is around) the river close to a little weir. This start leads to a bounce through the village, with limited headroom at the road bridge. Then a sharp turn to the right follows and the gorge begins – 2km of excitement. The road is high up on the right side. The gorge ends at Pont Ystumanner and the river calms down, and starts to meander. Less than 1km further, the Afon Cadair joins from the right. Although carrying less water, this river can be paddled from about 2km higher up, beyond Llanfihangel-y-pennant.

The river then bends to the left, heading south-west towards the sea. After a farm track bridge, it is 2km to the next road bridge, Pont-y-garth. Craig yr Aderyn is visible on the left side of the valley and looks very impressive from the water. Immediately below the bridge there is a small split weir with a tributary stream joining from the right.

The next stretch runs dead straight and looks canalised. There are three more small weirs not far ahead, which follow in quick succession. All are small, rocky constructions, and the third is said to have a noticeable stopper in high water.

The valley opens out, and the river winds in large bends, with a few islands, a sure sign that it is running out of steam, and soon to join the sea. Buildings are visible to the right, then Bryncrug village to the left, as the mountains to the south drop down to the coastal plain.

Pont Dysynni has plenty of parking by the old bridge, which is used by walkers and cyclists.

Variation

If you wish to continue down the river, the tidal part starts 1km downstream. The river winds among rushes and islands. After a short distance, the estuary opens out into Broad Water, a lagoon with marshy edges. The egress is river left onto a beach by a metal tubular footbridge, just before the railway bridge (SH 567 029) where there is plenty of parking. There is a tidal rapid below this egress point at low tide.

Small rapids on the Dyfi

13 River Dyfi

 **OS Sheets 124 and 135 | Aberangell to Machynlleth | 16km**

Shuttle	10 miles, via the A489 and A470, 15min
Start	Aberangell, SH 846 100
Finish	Machynlleth Bridge, SH 743 018

Introduction

The valley of the Dyfi is a rich pastoral area, with mountains to the north-east and a beautiful coastline where the river enters Cardigan Bay at Aberdyfi. The river rises at the junction of several small streams on the east flank of Aran Fawddwy, near the border between Gwynedd and Powys. The river is whitewater down to Dinas Mawddwy and Minllyn, and has further falls below Mallwyd, where there is a grade 3 gorge. There is a high bridge over the gorge but no access to the river. The river becomes tidal a few kilometres after Machynlleth.

Machynlleth is a tourist centre, and the major town hereabouts. It is a well-known cultural centre, the site of Laura Ashley's first shop, and home to the Museum of Modern Art. Welsh is widely spoken, and said to be understood by more than fifty per cent of the population.

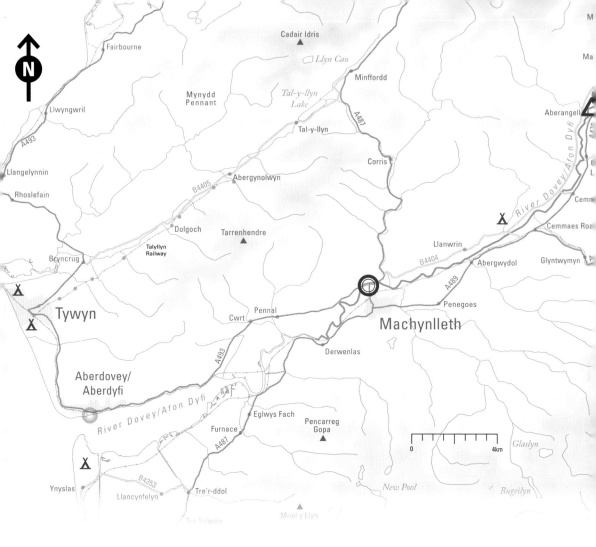

Just north, is the world-famous Centre for Alternative Technology (CAT), established some forty-five years ago in a former slate quarry. I highly recommend a visit. It is very interesting and much of the present wind and water power technology in the UK was developed here.

In the past, the area was a centre for copper mining, and the location for Owain Glyndwr's first 'parliament' in 1404. In 1644 during the English Civil War, the Roundheads won a battle against the local Royalists, and afterwards burned many of the fine houses owned by the landed gentry. The bridge at the end of the trip has existed since 1533. It was replaced in 1601, and rebuilt again for £250 in 1805.

Water level

This is a meandering river over a fairly flat valley, with shingle banks. The banks need to be covered for the level to be right for paddling. It is fairly obvious to see when the banks are exposed or covered from the road bridges, especially from the B4404 bridge.

River Dyfi Estuary

Campsites

There is a campsite just upstream from Mallwyd, another near Cemmaes Road and many more on the coast around Borth and Tywyn. The waterside caravan site at Aberangell does not allow camping.

Access and egress

Aberangell – SH 846 100

Cemmaes Bridge – SH 833 061

B4404 bridge, between Cemmaes Road and Llanwrin – SH 808 042

Machynlleth Bridge – SH 743 018

Description

At Aberangell, there is a waterside caravan site which provides at least pedestrian access onto the river. Make sure you ask for permission first. Parking is limited in the area, and cars may have to be left further back in the village.

The river has wide bends with gravel banks, similar to many other lowland rivers. The main road is always nearby, on the left bank. There is a minor road on the right bank. The valley gradually widens out as you progress downriver. Wildlife includes otters and herons.

After 5km the village of Cemmaes lies on the left bank, and there is a minor road bridge over the river. A further 4km and the River Twymyn, a fairly major tributary, joins the

Dyfi from the left, just before Cemmaes Road which is on the left side. Cemmaes Road is an important road junction with the A470 heading south-east to Newtown and the A489 heading down the valley.

The next bridge takes the B4404 over the river, which then follows the right bank. River right there is a large lay-by which could be useful if you wanted to take a larger group on the river for the final 7km down to Machynlleth. The valley is now quite broad and pastoral, with some large islands. The railway is tight on the left bank. The last part of the river is enjoyable, with mountains on both sides, and the vast Dyfi Estuary ahead.

At Machynlleth Bridge, egress is easy on the left bank, where there is a footpath. Parking is difficult, however. The best option is to leave vehicles near the railway station, 0.5km towards town, just beyond the railway bridge.

Variation

The Dyfi becomes tidal about 3km downstream, and there is scope for an estuary trip, but this requires careful planning. If you get it wrong, you may have to wade through treacherous mud or struggle paddling against the tide.

The main navigation issue is that the tides run fast and the sandbanks shift around. You will have to cover 6km in a fast-flowing narrow channel, and a further 7km to Aberdyfi in a wider channel. If you reach the tidal limit at high water, you will be going with the tide downstream and the 13km should take you around 2 hours. If you carefully follow the twisting channel, you could reach Aberdyfi with two thirds of the tide to go.

The estuary widens out to about 2km below Machynlleth Bridge, with large expanses of mud and sand. The Ynys Hir RSPB Reserve (one of the best in the UK) extends for most of the left side of the estuary, with no egress. The main A493 road comes close to the estuary at Aberdyfi.

High water at Aberdyfi is Dover HW -0320.

 Start point on the River Rheidol

14 Lower River Rheidol

⊔ ⊔ **OS Sheet 135** | **Capel Bangor to Aberystwyth** | **8.5km**

Shuttle	6 miles, via the minor road to the Rheidol Falls, and the A44 from Capel Bangor to Aberystwyth, 12min
Start	Footbridge, near Capel Bangor, SN 680 792
Finish	Bridge, Aberystwyth Industrial Estate, SN 610 804

Introduction

This is a lovely, easy canoe trip almost into the centre of Aberystwyth. The Lower Rheidol is a fast flowing river with many easy rapids. Although there are no difficult rapids, the flow can be strong, and it winds continuously between clumps of trees, and around gravel islands. Constant vigilance is required to spot obstacles such as fallen trees, and some of the bends are very tight. There are numerous places to stop on the trip down the river.

Aberystwyth is the largest market town on Cardigan Bay and the administrative centre for the county of Ceredigion. It is at a junction of tourist routes, and is well placed for spectacular Mid Wales to the east, Snowdonia to the north, and Pembrokeshire to the

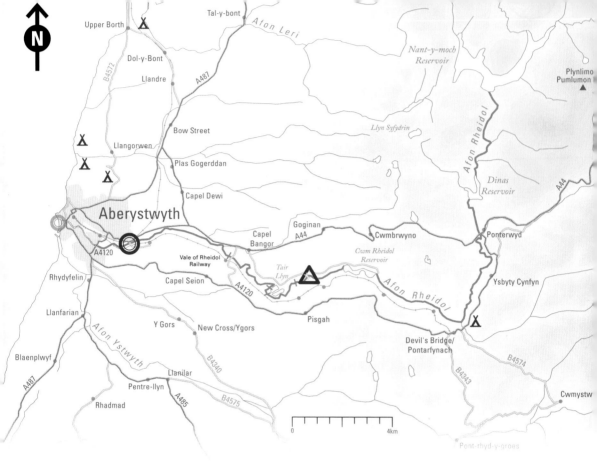

south. The university has a student body of 15,000, which doubles the town's population for nine months of the year. Historical interests include a castle and a Victorian-built cliff railway on Constitution Hill at the north end of town.

Water level

It is nearly always possible to paddle the lower Rheidol, as the dams upstream release water constantly to generate electricity. The river braids in its lower reaches, giving a choice of channels.

Campsites

There are a number of campsites near Devil's Bridge, and around Aberystwyth.

Access and egress

Access: from the A44, just east of Capel Bangor, take the minor road to Glan Rheidol and the Rheidol Falls. Access is by the footbridge over the river and there is ample parking (SN 680 792).

Egress: from the A44, heading east out of Aberystwyth, turn right over the bridge into the industrial estate. Park on the south side of the bridge, by a picnic spot (SN 610 804).

Access to the river is possible at other points.

Description

The river flows fast, and has sweeping bends from the start. After 1km, around a right-hand bend, there is a long rapid, followed immediately by a left-hand bend. From this bend, it is possible to **inspect** the next section which is right by Abernant Farm on the left bank. The river drops over rocks; in low water, this can be walked over, in high water it is more of a fall.

The river then takes almost a circular track around a large body of water, Tair Llyn. The railway is now alongside on the left bank and follows the river into Aberystwyth.

As the river follows a long bend to the right, there are two more fairly long rapids. There is then a very sharp bend to the left, almost a hairpin, and the road is above, on the right side of the river. The water here is swirly and confused, often disappearing into trees. The river meanders more, through large shingle banks and islands.

Next, a road bridge (linking Capel Bangor to the A4120) is followed by small rapids and shallows. After this the river is quite straight, but with a surprisingly large example of an oxbow lake. This is a crescent-shaped lake (often temporary) that is formed when a meander of a river is cut off from the main channel.

You then come to a split, take the left branch if possible. If the water is comparatively high, the main current will be in the left channel, but in low water this branch can look like a giant shingle bank, so take the right channel. The right has more bushes and trees, and may be blocked in places.

Just before the end of the trip, the two parts of the river recombine, and from then on the Rheidol is constricted to a man-made bed. The egress is easy, on the left bank just before the road bridge where there is car parking and a picnic area.

Variation

If you want to continue down into Aberystwyth, it is 2km to the tidal limit, almost under the A4120 bypass bridge, which is too high for access, then it is a further 2km to the sea, passing right through the middle of the town.

The Upper Rheidol

The Rheidol River is formed by streams rising on the sides of Plynlimon, also the source for the Severn and the Wye. This area has been chosen as one of three experimental release sites for the European beaver in Wales.

The Upper Rheidol has a fearsome reputation among paddlers. The headwaters have been dammed to form the Nant-y-Moch Reservoir, one of the largest in Wales. Below the reservoir, the river flows south, passing through the smaller Dinas Reservoir, and then entering a series of spectacular gorges. At the aptly named Devil's Bridge, the Mynach Falls enter from the south side of the gorge, providing a spectacular view and drawing many tourists. The narrow-gauge Vale of Rheidol Railway also finishes here after a laborious climb up from Aberystwyth.

A couple of miles downstream, the river flows over the Rheidol Falls, a hydro-electric scheme, and enters a reservoir with another dam a mile lower down. Once released, the river is flat and mature and winds down the valley to the start of the route described.

 Typical rapid – River Ystwyth

15 Lower River Ystwyth

  OS Sheet 135 | **Wenallt to Rhydyfelin** | **15km**

Shuttle	9 miles from Aberystwyth via the A487, A485, B4576, and a minor road back to Wenallt, 15min
Portages	Possibly one at a weir (SN 590 773) about 0.5km above Llanfarian Bridge
Start	Ford at Wenallt, SN 673 716
Finish	Road bridge at Rhydyfelin, SN 588 787

Introduction

The Lower Ystwyth is one of two rivers draining the hills to the east of Aberystwyth. The trip is through pleasant, rather than spectacular, countryside, but the reward is the university town of Aberystwyth at the end, a destination in its own right. The river maintains its flow right to the end with small, interesting rapids all the way down. The OS map does not show all the bends in the river, and online satellite 'Google' images are useful to see the actual contours. It is an ideal starter river for open canoe paddlers wishing to try small rapids.

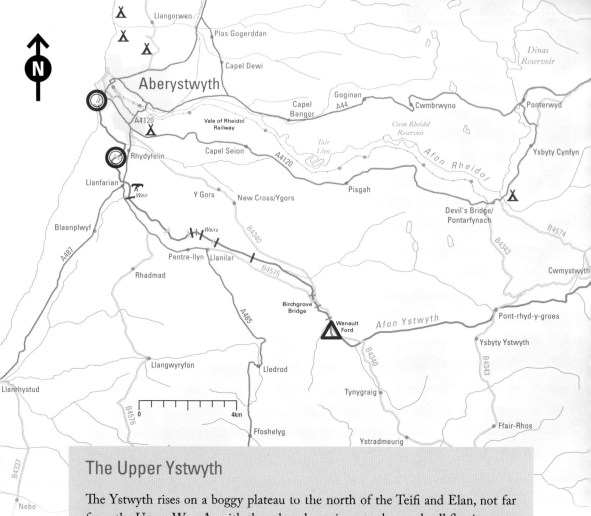

The Upper Ystwyth

The Ystwyth rises on a boggy plateau to the north of the Teifi and Elan, not far from the Upper Wye. As with the other short rivers to the north, all flowing west to Cardigan Bay, the Ystwyth has a very steep upper section. It drops through Pont-Rhyd-y-Groes, the only large village in the upper valley and flows through thick woodland making physical access to it difficult. From here, down to the road bridge above Wenallt, there is a grade 3/4 gorge. The Ystwyth then flattens out for its last stage to the sea.

Water level

The river can be paddled at low levels, but it is better when the gravel rapids are covered. From Birchgrove Bridge, it is possible to view the grade 2 rapid upstream on the bend and also the small rapids downstream.

Campsites

There is a site just off the A487 when entering Aberystwyth. There are others nearby and on the coast to the west.

Access and egress

Wenallt, at the ford – SN 673 716

Birchgrove Bridge – SN 666 729

Llanilar Bridge – SN 618 756

Rhydyfelin Bridge – SN 618 756

Description

The ford at Wenallt offers easy access. Please park with care so as not to obstruct; there isn't much space for vehicles and the roads are narrow both sides of the river.

There are easy rapids for 2km to Birchgrove Bridge, near Trawsgoed. The bend just upstream of the bridge has a good grade 2 rapid. There is a possible access point upstream of the bridge, river left, from a picnic spot with parking, but it is steep down to the river.

More easy rapids follow. The countryside flattens out, and the river runs almost dead straight for 3km. It has possibly been canalised at some time in the past. There are large gravel islands on this stretch, and more interesting, three small rocky weirs. The first weir is about halfway down this long stretch, and the second just before a footbridge. The third weir is before a left-hand bend. It is followed by a rapid before a right-hand bend, and then by a broken weir. All three should present no problem and are easily seen ahead. They will be covered in high water, but a bit of a scrape in low water.

At Llanilar Bridge, access is possible river right, upstream of the bridge, but parking is scarce.

The river then twists around many bends, and there is a minor road bridge about 1km after Llanilar Bridge. Some bends after this are very sharp, with overhanging trees and gravel rapids. Next is a **weir** of note (SN 590 773); it is 2.5km after the minor road bridge, and about 0.5km before the busy Llanfarian Bridge. It is possible to **portage** among the trees on either side. In low water it is easy to stop and **inspect** this **double drop** before running it. The author has not shot the weir in high water, but judges it to be potentially **dangerous**. It is safer to **portage** if in any doubt.

Llanfarian Bridge is high above the river, and does not offer any access. You are now in the environs of the town of Aberystwyth, still a pleasant area. In under 2km, you arrive at the bridge at Rhydyfelin, and the egress is downstream of the bridge, river left, up onto a footpath. Parking should be possible on the left side of the river.

Variation

An alternative is to paddle on 2.5km to the sea, at Aberystwyth's harbour. The Ystwyth joins the River Rheidol which is more apparent within the town. This part is flat, and can be shallow at low tide. There is a tidal weir about halfway down at the tidal limit. This extension to the trip may be a bit tedious, but you finish in the centre of Aberystwyth, with road access and parking.

South West Wales

South West Wales (Carmarthenshire, Ceredigion and Pembrokeshire) contains two of the longest rivers in Wales, the Teifi and the Tywi. It also has one of the most beautiful coastlines in the UK.

The landscape is one of low hills, rolling green fields and long wooded river valleys. The Tywi is a good touring river with great scenery, while the estuary offers very different canoeing. The West Cleddau, when in condition, gives good sport and the Teifi, to the north, flows through a beautiful valley. Nearby are the surfing beaches of Cardigan Bay, a veritable paddler's paradise.

Further south, the massive inlet of Milford Haven stretches far inland with its long estuarine tentacles and forms an unusual landscape. The town of Milford Haven has played an important role in forming the character of the area, both in the past as a welcome shelter for ships, and more recently as a centre for the oil industry. The towns of Pembroke Dock and Neyland, surrounding the Haven, are also quite industrial. The outskirts, however, give way very quickly to quiet countryside and peaceful villages. The market and tourism centre of Haverfordwest is just to the north.

The coast offers sea kayaking and surfing. Tenby and Saundersfoot have been well-known holiday destinations since the 1950s, popular with people from the English Midlands. The Pembrokeshire Coast Footpath runs through the linear national park and takes walkers and other outdoor lovers from Amroth near Tenby around the coast, past the Haven to Broad Haven, St David's, Fishguard and Newport, finishing at St Dogmaels near Cardigan. The whole stretch has some fabulous sandy beaches, and a generally mild climate.

The area offers much for tourists, and for lovers of castles in particular. Pembrokeshire is especially well endowed with ruins, but also with a few lived-in fortresses. Roch near Haverfordwest, Carew near Pembroke, and Manorbier on the coast near Tenby are great examples. Pembroke is a pretty town and has its own castle, towering above the streets.

Castles also abound in both the Teifi and Tywi valleys. The Teifi has an unusual flattish upper valley, with a meandering river and a large area of marsh. The middle section has some major and exciting rapids, and the lower part (two-thirds of the valley) has several small pretty towns, a remarkable gorge section near its end, and the very attractive town of Cardigan near the coast.

By contrast, the Tywi is a quiet river, with the small towns of Llandovery and Llandeilo, and the major regional centre of Carmarthen at the tidal limit.

Newcastle Emlyn Rapids, River Teifi

Cenarth Falls, River Teifi

16 Upper River Teifi (WW)

OS Sheets 135, 145 and 146 | **Llanfihangel-ar-arth to Cenarth** | **26km**

Shuttle	About 20 miles, via A484, A486, and B4336, 45min
Portages	Two possible, at Pont Allt-y-Cafn, and Henllan
Start	Llanfihangel-ar-arth, SN 456 402 or Llandysul Paddlers HQ, SN 414 402
Finish	Cenarth, SN 269 415

Introduction

The Teifi is the longest river flowing entirely within Wales, some one hundred and ten kilometres from its source in the Teifi Pools, high up on barren moorland, to the sea at Cardigan. In the 1960s and 70s, as paddlers pushed the boundaries of what was possible, it became a favourite touring river, in spite of difficult rapids in five locations, entailing tiring portages. This made the trip in either a soft-skinned or fibreglass boat an epic.

The Teifi is highly unusual in that it starts in a bog, flows slowly for many miles, and then accelerates in its lower reaches. The higher sections are well worth visiting for the scenery and wildlife. It is a small river until after the Cenarth Falls, then the volume increases and it flows through a beautiful valley, especially in the lower stretches.

At weekends in good weather, the river can be quite crowded.

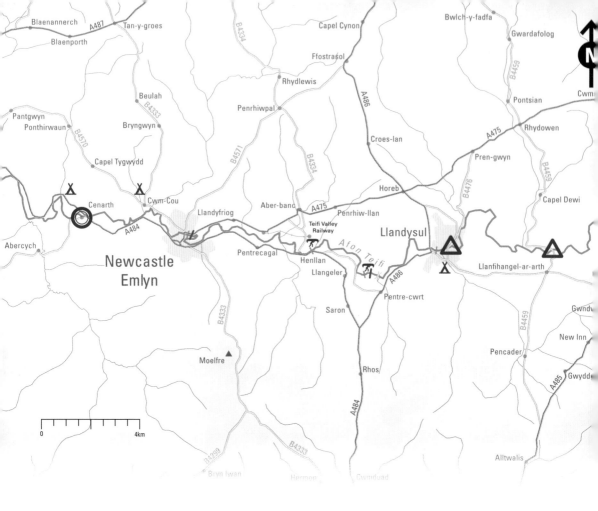

Water level

Llandysul is a good place to view the river. The section downstream of the village should be easily paddled without too many rocks.

Campsites

There are campsites at Llandysul, Aberhalen, near Newcastle Emlyn, and on the coast near Cardigan.

Access and egress

Sadly, the actions of salmon anglers on the river have restricted paddling greatly, and so the section described below, although fabulous, is only possible on some dates each year outside of the fishing season.

Llandysul Paddlers run a 'Teifi Tour' each October. They also run courses on the river, including padding down to Henllan several times a year. For more information: www.llandysul-paddlers.org.uk, tel. (01559) 363209, e-mail: bpaddlers@aol.com.

Llandysul slalom course, River Teifi

Physical access, often on tiny roads with many tight bends and very inadequate parking, can also be problematic. Access at the bridge at Llanfihangel-ar-arth can be tight for parking. If you cannot find parking there, then start at Llandysul Paddlers HQ. The last section of the river, being mainly tidal, is not affected, and is described in Section 17 of this book.

Llanfihangel-ar-arth – SN 456 402

Llandysul Paddlers HQ – SN 414 402

Henllan Bridge – SN 355 400

Newcastle Emlyn (the rugby club above town) – SN 314 407

The finish to this trip is when Cenarth Falls come into sight, with the Cenarth road bridge visible just downstream of the falls. The landing is onto a rocky, low, right-hand bank. There is a fairly long carry over rocks to reach a paying car park just upstream of the bridge (SN 269 415).

Description

The first 6km down to Llandysul has small rapids and a good flow. The river turns in a large semi-circle to the east, then back to the west. When the village of Llandysul comes into sight, the river bends away to the left, with playing fields in between. If you want to **stop and look** before the long Llandysul Rapids, egress on the left bank. A short walk will take you to the first bridge, and the HQ of Llandysul Paddlers. The river falls through rocky gaps, and the last gap in the 1km stretch is the most awkward, but nearly always grade 1/2, and only grade 3 in high water.

The canoe slalom course is obvious on the first stretch below the bridge, it has been used continuously since the mid-1960s.

The second bridge carries a fairly new road. Paddle 4km between wooded banks until you see the next (third) bridge, Pont Allt-y-Cafan (SN 386 392). A **dangerous weir**, which has caused fatalities, is obvious just below the bridge. Just before the bridge, the river bends left then right. The **portage** is on the right bank, preferably before the bridge. There are some good rapids below the weir.

It is 4.5km to Henllan Rapids which are a good grade 3/4 stretch. Prior **inspection** would be very wise. It is possible to park (with care) on the road leading up to Henllan village. **Portage** is possible along the rocky bank, river right, but the return to the river is only possible at the bridge at the end of the rapids, which carries the road up to Henllan village. Paddling these rapids the river picks up speed in a wooded gorge which leads to a large waterfall, down which you will be hurtled with little warning; first right, then left, with a rock in the middle.

The river quietens down again for 6km until above Newcastle Emlyn, the largest town in the valley. The river appears to almost enter the town, and then bends very sharply to the right in a very tight bend. As it turns to the left again, the rugby club is obvious on the right bank, with egress to the public road, where there is parking. Don't take vehicles into club grounds without asking. Egress here to avoid the final section which includes salmon steps graded 4/5 in high water.

Around the bend are the salmon steps, which in high water are awesome. They can be run on the right in medium to high water, but not in low water. There are then continuous rapids down to the bridge in the town.

From Newcastle Emlyn, it is 5.5km to Cenarth, and the Teifi becomes a slower, mature river. The falls at Cenarth can be heard some distance away. Land on the right bank before the falls. Carry your canoe over flat rocks to a paying car park. The spot is very popular with tourists, and coracles are often paddled here, offering rides for a fee.

 River Teifi at Cenarth

17 Lower River Teifi and Estuary

OS Sheet 145 | Cenarth to Towyn | 17.5km

Shuttle	10 miles, back up either side of the estuary on B roads to Cardigan, and then A484 to Cenarth, 10 miles, 30min
Start	Cenarth, SN 269 415
Finish	Towyn Warren Point, on the east side, SN 162 485 or Poppit Sands on the west side of the estuary, SN 156 483

Introduction

The Teifi is over one hundred kilometres long and enters the sea beyond Cardigan. There are various levels of whitewater along its length. The section chosen for this trip is very laid-back and enjoyable with no difficulties. It is suitable for relatively inexperienced open canoe paddlers and provides a good introduction to estuary paddling. The egress is quite easy.

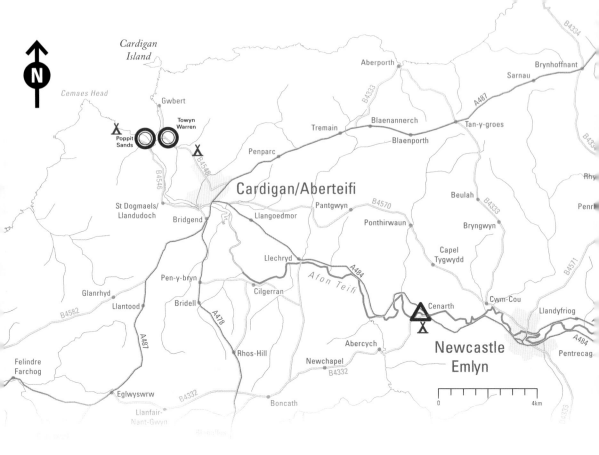

The sandy estuary is pleasant, and popular with holidaymakers. The lovely small towns of Newport, Aberporth, Newquay, Aberaeron and Cardigan are nearby, though Cardigan becomes very crowded in good summer weather. It is well provided with cafés, pubs and restaurants, and the castle is worth visiting.

Water level

The lower part of the Teifi is paddleable in all conditions, apart from just above Cardigan at low tide. Aim to arrive at the tidal part in the Cilgerran Gorge just before high water (the tide will be nearly slack an hour before), as this will give you two hours to paddle the 8km down to the egress and a landing without too much sand or mud to wade through.

High water at Cardigan is Dover HW -0405.

Campsites

There are campsites at Cenarth, and on the coast around Cardigan.

Access and egress

Start at Cenarth (SN 269 415), the river is accessed just below the bridge where there is a public car park. It will be crowded at weekends and bank holidays.

© River Teifi Estuary

Finish at Towyn Warren Point (SN 162 485) on the east side of the estuary. Take the B4548, which follows the estuary to Gwbert. At the obvious large boat club between the road and the water, take a lane down the side to the beach and parking. The only snag might be a very high tide, which could flood the car park!

Alternatively, finish at Poppit Sands (SN 156 483) on the west side. Take the B4546 through St Dogmaels to Poppit Sands. There is parking near the IRB station. A well-defined footpath through gorse leads to the very large sandy beach. The only drawback is the 400m walk to the car park carrying canoes or kayaks.

Other possible access points:

Llechryd (not much parking at this bridge) – SN 217 436

Cilgerran (steep and narrow road leading down from the village to good car parking and access to the river, signposted 'Teifi Walks') – SN 220 449

Cardigan (by Co-op supermarket) – SN 176 459

Description

The turbulent water caused by the falls above the bridge is just starting to calm down. The river makes a large bend to the right, following the main A484 road. Then there is an island and a sharp bend back to the left. The river winds around a high bluff on the right, and then the valley widens out. Llechryd Bridge is obvious, and any parking places will be on the left bank where a minor road heads back upriver, and a hotel entrance is downriver. The village is well back on the right bank.

The river leaves the road, and enters a deep wooded gorge for 5km. The Teifi defies 'normal' river behaviour; instead of a long meandering estuary, it has dug itself a narrow gorge, interesting to paddle through, and without difficulty. Cilgerran village and castle are high up on the left side.

The estuary leaves the gorge, and there is just over 1km of shallow water before the new road bridge at Cardigan. The castle is obvious high on the right bank, guarding the town, and houses appear, painted in bright pastel colours.

The former road bridge is now ahead, and egress is possible downstream on the right bank – either up a slipway at the start of the car park, or a bit further downstream. It is also possible to land on the opposite bank at the outdoor centre, a former warehouse. The river widens, bends left, and then right, for the remaining 4km to the egress. The channel is on the left side. There is a picnic spot about halfway down on the left bank.

Ahead, the channel narrows, and the left bank becomes marshy. There is a choice of egresses. Towyn Warren Point is on the right; as you draw level with the masts of the boat club, take the small shallow channel leading off to a convenient floating pontoon, very near to the car park.

If landing at Poppit Sands, follow the channel past Towyn Warren for a short way until it bends to the right. The sands are on the left and the breaking bar can be seen ahead. Don't go any further as the estuary entrance has a **dangerous bar**, possibly lethal to small boats in the wrong conditions.

Variations

To paddle the river only, exit at Cilgerran Gorge. There is a very convenient car park and picnic spot just where the river becomes tidal. The river section is 9.5km long. To paddle the estuary, launch at Cilgerran Gorge for an 8km tidal outing.

18 River Gwili (WW)

OS Sheets 159 and 145 | Cynwyl Elfed to Carmarthen | 10.5km

Shuttle	7 miles via A484
Portages	Possibly the rapid after Bronwydd Arms
Start	The Blue Bell Inn, Cynwyl Elfed, SN 373 275
Finish	Pont Abergwili, A485 Carmarthen, SN 430 218

Introduction

Rising in the ancient Glyn Cothi Forest, the River Gwili cuts through a steep, wooded valley before flowing into the Tywi just upstream of Carmarthen. The order of the day on this river is exciting whitewater touring through a beautiful forested valley.

Glyn Cothi, now part of Brechfa Forest, has supplied timber building materials since the 6th century. More recently, the area has been developed into a tourism destination and offers trails for walking, horse riding and cycling, including three mountain bike-specific trails.

As you paddle the river, you will pass White Water Consultancy in Bronwydd. The business was set up originally by Huw Evans in 1986. The first shop, little more than a tin shed, was in Llandysul, a major centre for paddlers on the River Teifi. Over the years it grew to become an importer and distributor of canoe gear and moved to these premises in 2000. It is well worth popping in to chat about local paddling opportunities and maybe even grab a deal on some new gear. The staff are very helpful.

Carmarthen is the main centre in this part of Wales, particularly for farming and tourism. To the west are the hills of Mynydd Preseli, the origin of the stones for Stonehenge.

Railway enthusiasts will be pleased to know that the Gwili Steam Railway, part of the former Carmarthen to Aberystwyth line that closed in 1965, follows the river for part of the section described. A selection of steam locomotives runs all year round and there are regular special events.

Water level

Information about water levels is available from www.rainchasers.com. The level on the gauge needs to be a minimum of 0.9. The rapid by the White Water Consultancy shop in Bronwydd gives a good indication of the level.

Campsites

There is a campsite at Nant, to the east of Carmarthen, and plenty more to the west and south on the Pembrokeshire coast.

Access and egress

Start at the Blue Bell Inn, Cynwyl Elfed (SN 373 275). Behind the inn there is a small bridge over the Afon Duad (a tributary). Cross the bridge and put in upstream, from the footpath.

Finish at Pont Abergwili, A485 Carmarthen (SN 430 218). Just before the large road bridge, take out on the right-hand side and follow the path to the road. There is plenty of parking on the old disused bridge downstream.

Description

The start is actually on the Afon Duad. After 1km it runs into the River Gwili. The Gwili itself begins quite narrow and with a bit of flow can be exciting, dodging rocks and negotiating the tight little rapids. It is like this for the first 2km until another small tributary joins from the left-hand side. The flow increases and the river widens.

Then follows several kilometres of meandering, through pretty woodland with easy grade 2 rapids. There are rocks to avoid, and in higher water, bouncy wavetrains to enjoy.

These rapids are interspersed with flat sections, allowing you to catch your breath and recover composure in between. The road is always close by, but not so much that it intrudes on the feeling of solitude.

The Gwili Steam Railway begins to follow the river. Starting on the left bank it soon crosses and winds its way through the valley, occasionally passing right next to the river. If you are lucky you will be treated to the sight of a magnificent old steam locomotive roaring up the valley with smoke billowing from its funnel.

The rapids continue, with one which is a little steeper than the others ending with a nice hole which can be quite good for surfing at some water levels. The banks are lined with trees; inspection would be difficult and not much can be seen from the river.

White Water Consultancy is 200m further on, a large building on the left with canoes and kayaks in the yard.

The rapid after the shop provides some nice waves and eddies to make, above and below the bridge. In higher levels some good little surf waves form here with great eddy service. This is an ideal practice site to stop at with a group.

The next kilometre takes you through the village of Bronwydd Arms, followed by more easy rapids. The village is soon left behind and after a few more bends comes the main rapid of the river; a ledge drop and a narrow chute. It is straightforward but in decent flows is probably approaching grade 3 (SN 424 224). The rapid is easily **inspected** from, or **portaged**, on the right bank. Below is a large pool which is perfect for clearing up any mishaps.

After this, it is a few hundred metres of flat water to the egress, on the right, before the A485 road bridge. Follow the obvious footpath up to the road.

19 River Tywi

OS Sheets 146 and 159 | Dolauhirion Bridge, Llandovery to Dryslwyn Castle | 35km

Shuttle	16 miles, via the A40 and minor roads at the start and finish
Portages	One possible, near the start
Start	Dolauhirion Bridge (1 mile north of Llandovery), SN 762 361
Finish	Dryslwyn Castle, SN 552 202

Introduction

The Tywi ('Towy' in English) is a major river in South West Wales, flowing south-west from the central mountains. The headwaters are trapped in Llyn Brianne, a long, snaking artificial lake which, unlike the Elan Valley reservoirs which were built to supply water to Birmingham, was constructed to control the whole river flow and enable extraction downstream. In the 1970s, shortly after completion, kayakers shot the very long spillway (illegally).

The fourteen kilometres-long upper section of the Tywi includes several grades of difficult whitewater. By the time it reaches Llandovery, and the start of our trip, it has changed in nature and become a much milder waterway in a flat-bottomed valley.

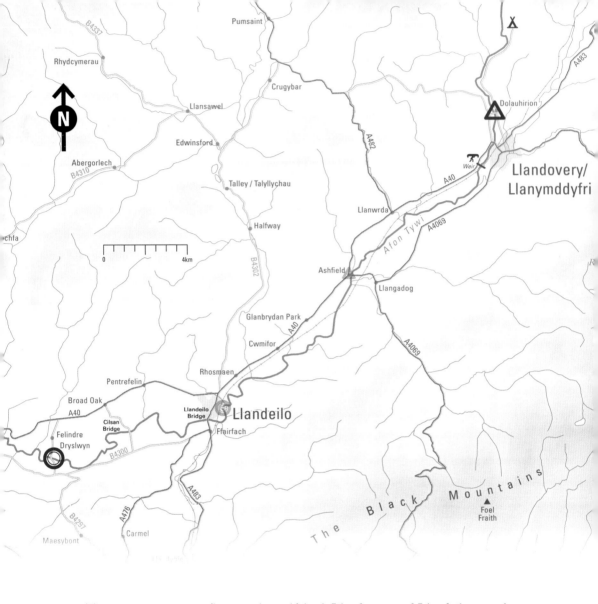

The river passes near to (but not through) both Llandovery and Llandeilo, two pleasant market towns, and flows for forty-five kilometres through a very quiet agricultural valley (it is possible not to see anybody all day while paddling) until it becomes tidal near Carmarthen, the county town, and an important market and route centre. The tidal stretch is described in Section 20 of this book.

Water level

The minor gravel rapids should be covered when seen from the road up the valley.

Campsites

There are sites at Quarry Lodge, White Mill, both near Carmarthen, and Erwlon, Llandovery.

Access and egress

Dolauhirion Bridge (one mile north of Llandovery) – SN 762 361. (There is no parking at Dolauhirion Bridge, please off-load canoes and remove vehicles to Llandovery.)

Ashfield Bridge – SN 695 286

Llandeilo Bridge – SN 627 219

Dryslwyn Castle – SN 552 202

Description

At Dolauhirion Bridge, access the river from the path on the left bank, downstream of the bridge.

There are small, playful grade 2 rapids downstream, and the river is fairly straight for 1km. The road is on the right side, and the railway to the left.

At a sharp bend to the left, a railway bridge comes into sight. There is an awkward drop upstream of the bridge where the river appears to flow over what is possibly an old **weir** (SN 754 335), composed of large wooden stakes and boulders. It can be **difficult**, but it is possible to **portage**; the right bank is best.

After this, the river meanders more, and the Afon Dulais joins from the right near Llanwrda, the village on the right. The river then passes under the railway again, and Ashfield Bridge is soon reached. Access is possible river left, downstream of the bridge.

Llangadog is 2km away on the left. Occasional small rapids follow. The loops in the river are close to becoming oxbow lakes in places. These are crescent-shaped lakes (often temporary) that form when a meander of a river is cut off from the main channel.

Llandeilo is visible ahead, built on a defensive position on a hill to the right of the river. The railway line stays low down in the valley, alongside the river. Llandeilo Bridge is magnificent, but a long way from the town! Access here is river left, just after the bridge, onto a lane running down from the main road. It is possible that it originally was a ford. The lane is narrow, and parking is scarce. The walk to the main road is 400m, and even here there is no obvious parking, apart from along the road near Pont Gwladys Station.

After Llandeilo, the river slows down quite considerably, and flows in a giant semi-circle to the right, around the Newton House Estate. Two lakes flow into the Tywi from the right side, both look like oxbow lakes. A long bend to the left to Cilsan Bridge, then 6km of bends with a few islands, and the end of the trip comes into sight, the very obvious ruins of Dryslwyn Castle, high on a hill to the right. This last stretch, with many sand and gravel shallows, is good for finding hidden picnic places before the canoeing is over.

There is a large car park, picnic tables, and easy access off the river.

Dryslwyn Castle

Canny builders chose the site for this castle! Records show that it had been built by 1246, at a time of trivial skirmishes between the Welsh tribes. Less than two centuries later, by 1403, it had been decommissioned, and taken apart by English troops.

Variations

The 35km of this trip make it a long day for the inexperienced. It could be shortened by 10km, either by finishing at Llandeilo (please note that there is no parking at the bridge, and that it is a good 400m walk to the main road), or by starting at Ashfield Bridge, near Llangadog, where there is parking space for one vehicle only. An advantage of starting at Ashfield Bridge is that the optional portage below Llandovery is avoided.

An intrepid paddler could chose to continue down the beautiful estuary, a total distance of 70km. Please note that there is no access from the bridge at Llandilo-yr-ynys, near Nantgaredig as it is too high above the river, and that landing at Carmarthen is awkward, as the town is high above the muddy tidal river and there is only one obvious landing slip.

Muddy estuary, River Tywi

20 Tywi Estuary

OS Sheet 159 | **Carmarthen to Ferryside** | **14km**

Shuttle	10 miles along the A484 (potential train shuttle from Ferryside to Carmarthen)
Start	The Quay Centre, Carmarthen, SN 409 198
Finish	River Towy Yacht Club, Ferryside, SN 365 104

Introduction

The Tywi ('Towy' in English) runs out of Llyn Brianne, through the Cambrian Mountains, then flows south across farmland before becoming tidal just upstream of Carmarthen. It is the second longest river contained entirely within Wales.

This trip begins at the 17th-century port of Carmarthen ('Caerfyrddin' in Welsh), which boasts a rich and varied history. Near the start is a rare surviving example of a bascule bridge (or balance-operated drawbridge), completed in 1911. It hasn't opened since the 1950s and is a Grade II listed building.

At the mouth of the estuary, on the northern shore, is Llansteffan Castle, a Norman fort built in the 12th century, as part of the invasion of Wales. Opposite the castle is the small fishing village of Ferryside. Its speciality is cockles.

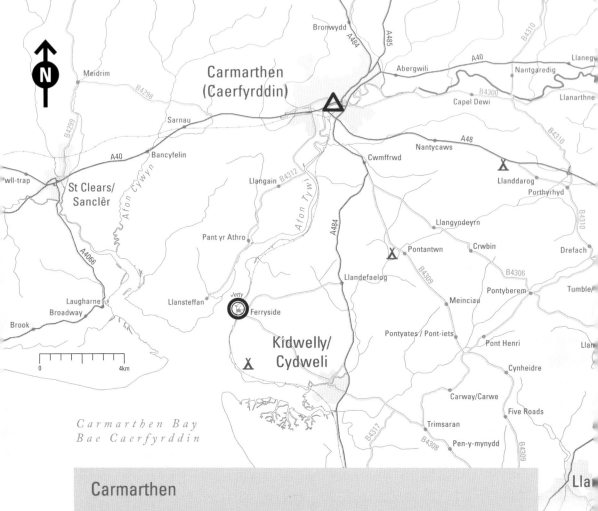

Carmarthen

Carmarthen was known as 'Moridunum' (sea fort) during the Roman occupation of Britain. It was the capital of the Demetae tribe.

A Norman castle was built in 1094, destroyed in 1215, and then re-built. Carmarthen was the first medieval town in Wales to have walls.

The Black Death, introduced through the shipping trade, brought devastation between 1347 and 1349.

The town developed shipbuilding and outfitting as well as imports of iron, lead, wine, brass goods, fruits and spices. By the 1720s the tonnage handled by the port was twice that of the Port of Cardiff.

Many of the locals, if not employed by the port or in shipping, were fisherman. They fished for salmon and sewin (sea trout) from handmade coracles, a practice that dates back certainly to Roman times and possibly even the Bronze Age.

Carmarthen is, by far, the largest town in this part of Wales, It is a very busy place in the summer. The A40 road around the town is a major artery from the Midlands and often has traffic jams during holiday times.

The wind can be strong on the estuary and it is important to check the forecast before setting off. If the forecast is for onshore winds, it may be prudent to do the trip in reverse, this would obviously have to be matched with an incoming tide.

Further down the estuary, after Ferryside, the open sea is not far away. There is a fearsome sandbar, not recommended for canoeing. Mariners are warned not to approach except between 3 hours either side of high tide at Carmarthen.

Water level

The estuary is best paddled in the top half of a falling tide. It is possible at lower levels but there is more likelihood of grounding on sand-bars. South-west winds may cause very strong tides down at Ferryside.

High water at Carmarthen is Dover HW -0455.

Campsites

There is a campsite at Nant, just west of Carmarthen and one south of Ferryside.

Access and egress

Start at Carmarthen – SN 409 198. Park in the Quay Centre car park and launch from the slipway just downstream.

Finish at Ferryside – SN 365 104. Park right outside the River Towy Yacht Club.

Description

The river quickly leaves the town behind and begins lazily weaving its way down through farmland. The flow is gentle except in times of flood and then only bridge stanchions pose a hazard.

The river flows between tree-lined banks for several kilometres, meandering slowly with small riffles here and there. There are a couple of islands, both of which are best passed to the left where the channel is deeper.

Along the river there are tall reedbeds, which are home to a host of wildlife, including otters. Beyond the beds, the wooded hillside is dotted with farms and houses. After several kilometres, the river widens and begins to feel like an estuary. At lower tidal levels it can become very shallow and careful navigation is required to avoid having to wade the boat. The sand is, however, quite firm and will take the weight of a person without the risk of sinking.

It is in this section that grey seals can be seen following salmon upriver for several miles. Cormorants also hunt for eels and small fish.

As you approach Towy Boat Club, you will see boats moored on the right. The club has a jetty (SN 365 125). The end of the trip is not much more than 1km further on. This is the widest part of the estuary so far and the open sea horizon can be seen in the distance.

Ferryside appears quickly on the left. Egress onto the sandy beach near the narrow, wooden jetty and walk up to the car park outside the River Towy Yacht Club (not to be confused with the previously mentioned Towy Boat Club). We highly recommend fish and chips (or a cake) at the Ferry Cabin Café, just around the corner next to the station.

© *Haverfordwest | istockphoto.com*

21 Western River Cleddau (WW)

OS Sheet 158 | Wolf's Castle to Haverfordwest | 15km

Shuttle	8 miles via A40
Start	Wolf's Castle, SM 956 263
Finish	Haverfordwest, SM 955 153

Introduction

The Western Cleddau is unusual in that its source is only four kilometres from the sea, near Fishguard, but it flows over thirty kilometres south in the opposite direction. Legend has it that Wolf's Castle is the site where the last wild wolf in Wales was slain.

The river cuts through hard, volcanic rock to form a steep-sided valley with several excellent bedrock shelf rapids, especially in the upper sections. There are several nice ledge drops and waves to play on, and it would make a great run for someone in their first stages of whitewater paddling. The difficulty never goes above grade 2 but in higher flows trees can be a **hazard** as the river is narrow throughout.

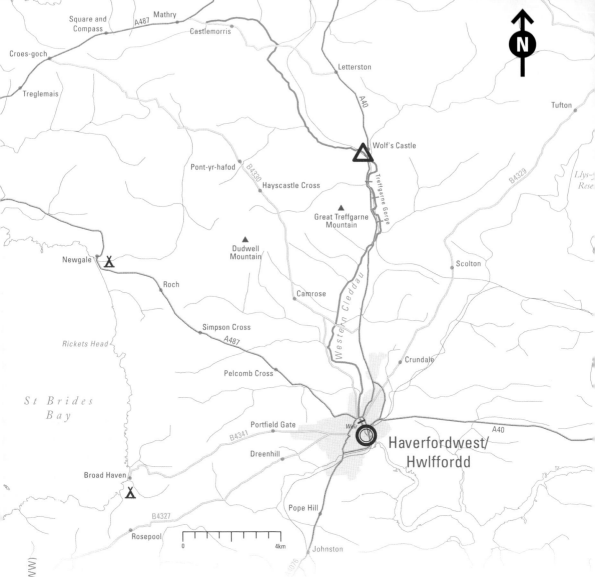

From the river you will be able to see the rhyolitic outcrops of Great Treffgarne Mountain. This is well worth walking up to if you have a free evening, to explore the rocks or do one of the easy climbs.

The river flows through Haverfordwest, a major town with an imposing castle. It isn't often that one paddles right through the centre of a town, being gawped at by tourists.

Beyond Haverfordwest, the Western Cleddau becomes tidal, and further south joins the Eastern Cleddau Estuary to form the Daugleddau, meaning 'two Cleddau' in Welsh (see Section 22).

Be sure to pick up any supplies you need in Haverfordwest as there isn't much in the village of Wolf's Castle.

Water level

Information about water levels on this section is available from www.rainchasers.com (search for Cleddau [Western]). A minimum level for this run would be 1.1 on the gauge. At 1.5 the trees begin to be a problem.

Campsites

There are sites on the coast to the west of Haverfordwest, near Broad Haven, and Newgale Sands, a fabulous surfing beach.

Access and egress

Start at Wolf's Castle – SM 956 263. From a large lay-by, next to a small village green, steps lead down to the river under the A40 road bridge.

St Catherine's Bridge – SM 945 198.

Finish at Haverfordwest – SM 955 153. A few hundred metres after the weir in Haverfordwest there is a slipway down to the river on the right-hand side.

Description

After launching you pass under the A40 and the fun starts immediately with a narrow, stream-like feel. After a hundred metres or so the River Anghof enters from the left-hand side and more or less doubles the flow. You are surrounded by trees and farms. There are no rapids as such, but the water is fast flowing and the twisty nature of the river requires concentration from the outset.

After 1.5km the river passes under the first railway bridge and enters the steep-sided Treffgarne Gorge; the road is visible on the right-hand side. This announces the first proper rapid which begins on the bend. It is straightforward and easily navigated. There follows a few more little rapids until you can see Great Treffgarne Mountain. A longer, boulder garden-style rapid then leads down to the second railway bridge. This is entertaining and technical at lower flows and is a solid grade 2 rapid if the river has some flow.

After this second bridge it really gets going, beginning with a series of four ledge drops which in higher water create excellent chutes and sometimes even playwaves; great fun and an excellent location to practise simple moving-water skills.

The river continues through a forested gorge with lots of easy rapids weaving around twisty bends. It is almost continuous for 5km until it goes under the A40 and the gradient flattens out.

The next few kilometres weave through pretty farmland and the banks are home to an abundance of wildlife including otters, kingfishers and lamprey. Despite having flattened out, the river's hurried pace continues through small, shingle rapids and very soon St

Catherine's Bridge (SM 945 198) is reached. This is over halfway and for those just after the excitement of the whitewater and the gorge, it provides an excellent alternative finish point.

More easy rapids follow and the pleasant countryside provides scenic touring. The good flow even in lower water levels is perfect for those wanting a relaxed day out.

Pretty soon the large medieval market town of Haverfordwest comes into view. There is a small gauging weir which is often covered. Another 1km and you are in the centre of town. It is difficult to believe that this is the same river as the one in the wild gorge further north.

The final hit of excitement comes in the form of a weir with a fish ladder in the centre, which is canoe friendly. This is straightforward and lots of fun. The water above the weir is slow moving and the weir is therefore easily **inspected** from the water. It is also a short walk from the finish, so when running the shuttle it is possible to walk up 100m and check it out.

After the weir and the obligatory photos have been taken, there is a slipway 100m further on the right. Walk up to the car park in front of the Bristol Trader pub, and maybe even enjoy a drink or a home-cooked meal before heading on to the next adventure.

 Hidden anchorage on Carew River

22 Daugleddau Estuary

OS Sheet 158 | Burton Ferry to Carew Castle | 9km

Shuttle	7 miles via A477
Start	Burton Ferry, The Jolly Sailor Inn, SM 978 049
Finish	Carew Castle car park, SM 042 039

Introduction

The Daugleddau Estuary is formed by four rivers; the Eastern and Western Cleddau, the Cresswell and the Carew. Beyond the A477 road bridge, the estuary opens out into the Milford Haven which has been important for shipping as far back as the 8th century, when Vikings sheltered their longboats here from fierce Atlantic storms. Today, it is the largest and busiest port in Wales.

The trip described in this section is within the Pembrokeshire Coast National Park, a much quieter and scenic stretch of water than the Haven, with plenty of history and wildlife. Starting at the small village of Burton, it explores inland, to the heart of the Daugleddau, including some of the more secluded backwaters. It continues all the way to the impressive Carew Castle and Tidal Mill.

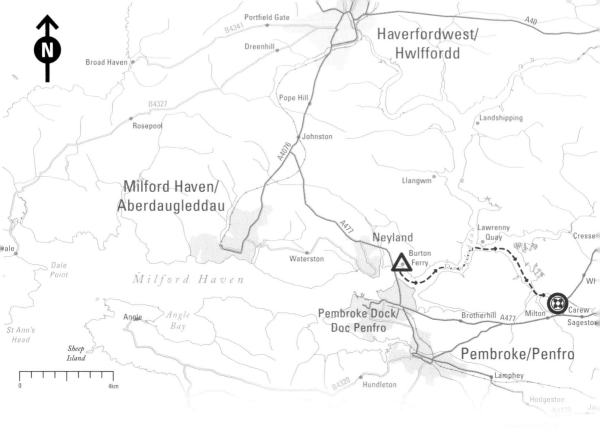

The castle was built in the late 13th century, on the site of a Norman fort dating from the early 1100s, as an addition to Edward I's chain of castles across North Wales. These strongholds for his army were ultimately used to gain a foothold in Wales, resulting eventually in the occupation of Wales by English forces. By the 17th century the castle had fallen into disrepair and was eventually abandoned. Since 1983 it has been managed by the Pembrokeshire Coast National Park and is well worth a visit.

Looking out to sea from Burton Ferry, you will see the Cleddau Bridge which opened in 1975. Before then, the only way across the bay was via a 30 mile journey inland or a ferry with a 24 vehicle capacity. Beyond the bridge is the busy scene of the industrial towns Neyland and Pembroke Dock. To the west are the oil refineries on both the north and south banks of the Haven. Pembroke Dock hides Pembroke, further south. This is a pity, because it is a pretty little town, with a fabulous castle right in the centre.

Access and egress

Start at Burton Ferry, The Jolly Sailor Inn – SM 978 049. A polite word and a promise to have a meal in the pub (strongly recommended) means you can use the car park for the day. Launch where the road is virtually at the water's edge.

Finish at Carew Castle car park – SM 042 039. Egress at the north end of the causeway by the tidal mill and walk 100m to the mill and castle car park.

Campsites

There are plenty of campsites on the coast to the south and west, near Tenby and St Davids and several near Haverfordwest.

Description

Head inland, away from the bridge, hugging the shore and around the point. Immediately the port and towns are left behind and you are surrounded by countryside. The small craggy cliffs on the left offer good protection from the wind.

Weave around moored boats of all shapes and sizes, and after about 1.5km there is a break in the cliffs and you will see Rudders Boatyard, the perfect pirate lair, hidden from prying eyes. More cliffs follow for another 200m before giving way to rolling farmland. Another 1km until you round a second point, and you are into the heart of the Daugleddau. This is the prettiest section with wooded shores and shingle beaches, watched over by 13th-century Benton Castle, painted white, now converted into a private house.

Off Jenkins Point, several hundred metres before the castle, you need to turn right into the channel leading into the Cresswell and Carew rivers. The channel narrows, and you pass Lawrenny Quay on the left; a few houses and a boatyard. Egress could be made here if the weather turns foul, though it's a long distance back to the start or to Carew!

Just after the jetty at Lawrenny Quay, is the wreck of the *Helping Hand*, a sailing trawler built in 1921, converted to diesel in 1933 and used for minesweeping around Milford Haven during World War Two. She was abandoned here around 1968, and has gradually broken apart with only the skeleton remaining.

From this point forward the water can be very shallow if the tide is out and the muddy shallows should be given a wide berth. About 1km after entering the channel there is a rock in the middle, the Black Mixen. Beyond it, the channel widens drastically and splits in two. Take the right-hand channel, heading south-east.

The West Williamson Quarries, now owned by the National Trust, are on the point between the two channels. They have become saltmarsh wetlands and a good place to see many species of birds including curlews, little grebes, mute swans and oystercatchers. With so many uncommon species of birds in the area, if you are quiet and explore the myriad of tiny inlets around the point, you may be treated to some rare sights!

Continue up the Carew River for 2km until it narrows to just 100m or so. There are several inlets off to the right, so staying on the left will guide you into the correct channel. After another 1km you will reach Carew Castle and Tidal Mill.

Take out at the northern end of the causeway. The millpond is a Site of Special Scientific Interest and boating activities are sadly not allowed. A footpath runs to the car park about 100m from the causeway.

Second drop, Upper River Usk

South Wales

South Wales is the most diverse of all of the sections in this book – stretching from near the English border, across the traditional mining valleys, to the cities of Cardiff and Swansea. However, finding suitable routes to include was difficult. Not only are the rivers technical, short, and run off quickly, the access, in tightly built villages which run ribbon-like along the valleys, can be awkward.

The M4 provides an easy corridor into South Wales; Newport near the border, then Cardiff, followed by Barry, Bridgend, Porthcawl, and Port Talbot with its steel works. After Swansea, the M4 becomes the A48 to Carmarthen and the sea beyond.

To the east, the Brecon area has a lot to offer paddlers; the River Usk, another long Welsh river, provides two easy whitewater trips described in the next two sections of this book. The Wye is only half an hour's drive north-east, and the Tywi is twenty or so miles west, on the A40 at Llandovery. There is also lovely canal which follows the Usk.

The Brecon Beacons National Park is a great area for outdoor activities, including walking, pony-trekking, climbing, caving and canoeing. South of the park are the parallel steep-sided valleys of carboniferous limestone, which provided Wales with most of its massive amounts of coal. To transport the coal to the coast, railways used to run down every valley to the ports.

These South Wales Valleys are well-known for difficult whitewater, because of the steep falls in the upper stretches, and the numerous weirs constructed to harness water power for industrialisation.

Nearby, in Cardiff, there is an artificial whitewater course, a great draw for paddlers looking for a reliable level of water. Further west is the Gower Peninsula, one of Wales' little-known playgrounds, with superb beaches, and paddling and surfing possibilities. Further north-west, the countryside changes dramatically to the lush greenness of Pembrokeshire, and many miles of fabulous coast.

Taking the first drop, Upper River Usk

23 Upper River Usk (WW)

 OS Sheet 160 | **Sennybridge to Brecon** | **14km**

Shuttle	9 miles, through Brecon onto the A40 to Sennybridge, 20min
Portages	There are three rocky falls in the first 2km, which are grade 2/3, in medium to high water. All can be portaged
Start	Sennybridge official access point, via a lane beside the Red Lion pub, SN 920 288
Finish	Brecon, Promenade car park, above Brecon Weir, SO 037 289

Introduction

The pleasant, unspoilt town of Brecon is a major market and farming centre, with many local and craft shops. At the confluence of the Usk and the Honddu rivers, Brecon has always been a route centre and has plenty of historical interest. It can get busy and the traffic may be a bit of a headache during summer holidays, despite the bypass on the other side of the river.

The Usk starts below its reservoir and remains tiny until Trecastle. Ten kilometres downstream at Sennybridge, the watercourse is joined by the Senni and becomes more of a river. From here, there is a lovely short trip, especially for canoes. There are no real

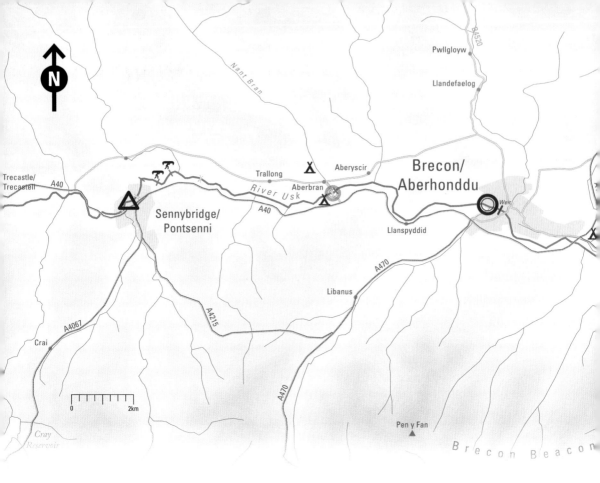

difficulties apart from three falls in the first two kilometres, and these can be portaged. With enough water, the rapids are easy and make the trip very enjoyable. Even in high water the rapids have large waves, but no other difficulties. The first few kilometres are in a high, wooded gorge, then the scenery opens out into more pastoral countryside.

Below Brecon, the river becomes a grade 3/4 torrent.

Water level

At the start at Sennybridge, there should be enough water to cover the rocks in the small rapids under the road bridge.

Information about water levels is available from www.rainchasers.com or www. riverlevels.uk. Enter 'Brecon' in the 'search' box to find the appropriate page. The level should be higher than 0.55.

Campsites

There are campsites just east of Brecon, west of Brecon, at Aberbran, and by the river at Crickhowell.

Access and egress

The Wye and Usk Foundation controls access on both rivers, and has provided designated access points. Please read the following information on the website:

http://www.wyeuskfoundation.org/navigation/index.php

Web cams can be found here:

http://www.wyeuskfoundation.org/conditions/index.php

On this stretch there are only three access points:

Sennybridge – driving through Sennybridge, the Red Lion pub is easy to find on the right side of the road. Turn right just before the pub, and drive down a narrow lane, which winds down towards the river. The launch field is signposted. There is ample parking (20–30 vehicles), and easy access onto the river (SN 920 288). In wet weather this green field can get very muddy. An alternative is to offload the canoes in the car park at the back of the pub, and then remove vehicles to the community hall car park a little back along the main road, up a hill on the south side (opposite side from the Red Lion) of the main road.

Aberbran – egress river left above the bridge, and carry across to the farm campsite, where there is parking on hard standing (for payment), and toilets – SN 986 291.

Brecon – Promenade car park. Head west out of town on the north side of the river, the car park is signposted. Large pay and display car park – SO 037 289.

Description

The Usk winds through Sennybridge between tree-lined banks; it is quite narrow along this section. The river drops over small rapids, and after 500m flows under a minor road bridge, and then bends left. Wooded sides rise steeply with no road access. The first **fall** is on a sharp right-hand bend, just visible from upriver. Landing can be made on the right bank, a few metres above the fall, and a walk to the bend on a footpath gives a good vantage point to **inspect**. It is best shot on the extreme right, near the bank. It has been run in other places, though this is made more difficult by small wooded islands, which guard the approaches, particularly the extreme left-hand side. A **portage** can be made along the inspection path, with access back onto the river a few metres downstream.

The second **fall** is 300m further on, and a bit more serious. It should be **inspected**, again from the right bank, landing about 50m upstream. It is possible to **portage** along the right bank. The left bank has a good path but it cannot be used to portage as the trees are overhanging. There is a chute near the left bank but it is overhung by trees. The fall is a sheer 1.5m, and is normally run about a third of the way out from the right bank. Open canoes shoot this at a 45° angle.

After 0.5km, the river leaves the gorge, and bends right and then sharp left. Land to **inspect** about 50m above the third **fall**, on the left bank this time. The fall can be **portaged** most easily on the left side, by climbing down a ladder on a small cliff, and lowering boats into the pool below the fall. In low water, the fall has to be taken on the left side over a vertical drop. In high water, the rocky and rather messy right side can be shot, but there are routes to suit all tastes.

The A40 main road is now present on the right bank. After the third fall, the river bends sharply to the right, and then the River Cilieni enters on the left side. The river flows down to a minor road bridge, the first of several small bridges on this section. It is then 4.5km down to the Aberbran Bridge. The River Nant Bran enters from the left immediately after the bridge, and almost into the quite heavy rapid just downstream.

The farm at Aberbran provides a camping and caravan site, and very useful parking close to the farmyard. Please do not try to shorten the distance to your vehicle by parking either at the first farm entrance, or on the road, as it causes obstruction. Finishing the trip here would cut off about 6km from the 14km total.

The river quietens down, and after Aberyscir on the left, where the River Ysgir joins from the left, it takes a large anti-clockwise bend around a wooded hill, with a final straight into Brecon. The finish point is at an obvious car park on the left bank, with a picnic site before it. The straight line of Brecon Weir can be seen ahead.

Variation

It is possible to continue down the Middle River Usk, described in the next section. Brecon Weir can be shot down the face, or portaged on the right bank.

24 Middle River Usk (WW)

 **OS Sheets 160 and 161** | **Brecon to Talybont-on-Usk** | **14km**

Shuttle	6 miles, back via the main A40 road, through the centre of Brecon, and minor roads to the Promenade car park, 20min
Portages	Possibly two; a sloping weir in Brecon, and a broken weir just after the canal aqueduct
Start	Brecon, the Promenade car park, SO 037 289
Finish	Road bridge on the Llansantffraed to Talybont-on-Usk road, just off the A40, SO 123 233

Introduction

This trip is good for relative beginner river paddlers (canoeists as well as kayakers), with easy rapids, some interesting water, and long sweeping bends near the finish.

The Monmouthshire and Brecon Canal is nearby. It finishes in the centre of Brecon at a basin overlooked by the theatre. The canal winds along the Usk Valley, through quiet and beautiful stretches which are worth visiting (and possibly paddling if the Usk is either too low or too high!).

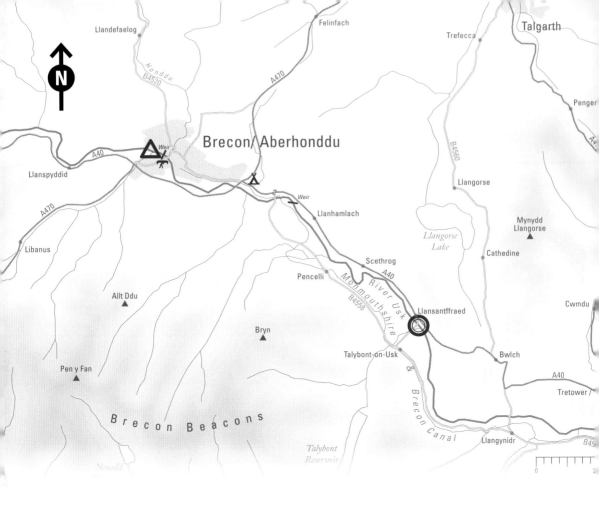

Water level

The shallows through Brecon must be covered.

Information about water levels is available from www.rainchasers.com or www.riverlevels.uk. Enter 'Brecon' in the 'search' box to find the appropriate page. The level should be higher than 0.55.

Campsites

There are campsites just east of Brecon, west of Brecon, at Aberbran, and near the river at Crickhowell.

Access and egress

The Wye and Usk Foundation controls access on both rivers, and has provided designated access points. Please read the following information on the website:

http://www.wyeuskfoundation.org/navigation/index.php

Web cams can be found here: http://www.wyeuskfoundation.org/conditions/index.php

On this stretch, there are only two access points, at the start and finish.

Start in Brecon, at the Promenade car park – SO 037 289.

Finish at the road bridge on the Llansantffraed to Talybont-on-Usk road, just off the A40 – SO 123 233.

When taking vehicles to the finish, the exit off the main A40 is a narrow right-hand turn (signposted to Talybont). The lane winds downhill around a hairpin bend to the valley floor. Parking is in a field on the right-hand side of the road after crossing the river bridge.

Description

This trip sets off from the large car park at the Promenade. Once on the water, you will immediately be faced by the large Brecon **Weir**, which can be taken either by scraping over the face, or via a chute on the left side. In high water, this weir should be treated with respect, and there is a fairly easy **portage** on the right side.

The town of Brecon is on the left side, and the suburb of Llanfaes on the right. After 1km the main road bridge in the town is reached, and just before this, the River Honddu joins from the left. In high water, the impact of the Honddu will be felt. The Usk tributaries are famous for their red colour in flood, due to the red soil washing off fields very rapidly. If the main river suddenly changes from black or brown to red, watch out, as the river is flooding!

The river winds in a long left-hand bend around the town and the A40 bypass is visible high up on the right bank, 3.5km after the town bridge.

The Monmouthshire and Brecon Canal is above the river on the left bank, and 1km after the bypass the canal crosses over the river on a stone aqueduct. There is a considerable rapid just below this, over a broken weir. The flow is heavy in flood.

The river is still following the A40, and the canal leaves to the right after 2km, towards the other side of the valley. The landscape becomes much flatter and the river flows through gentle farmland. In high water, the river widens out greatly over marshy ground. The egress is river right, just before the road bridge. Scramble up the bank to the field.

Variation

The next section of the river, through Llangynidr to Crickhowell, is not described in this book as it is much more difficult and there are access difficulties. However, accessing the river at either Crickhowell or, 4km further on, at Glangrwyney Bridge would give many more kilometres of paddling. It is possible to paddle 60km of grade 1 down to Abergavenny, Usk, Newbridge-on-Usk and Caerleon.

 © Monmouthshire and Brecon Canal, Llangynidr

25 Monmouthshire and Brecon Canal

Shuttle	About 13 miles one way, via the A4077 and A40 back to Brecon, 30min
Portages	Three portages: a first lock just over 3km from the start, four locks close together at Llangynidr, and one over an aqueduct, 1.5 km further on
Start	Brecon Canal basin, SO 048 281
Finish	Gilwern Marina, SO 243 146

Introduction

The Monmouthshire and Brecon Canal (called the 'Mon and Brec') is a very pleasant and quiet canal, winding its way past the back of houses in Brecon, shadowing the River Usk, first on the north side, and then crossing the river via an aqueduct to the south side. It finally leaves the river after Abergavenny and heads south. The long, shaded, leafy sections provide a peaceful canoe trip.

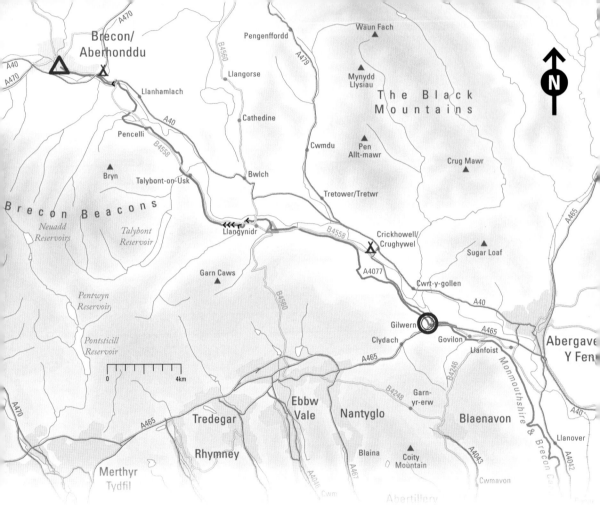

It used to be called the Brecknock and Abergavenny Canal, and joined the Monmouthshire Canal at Pontymoel, south of Pontypool. The southerly section going into Newport had thirty locks but was closed to traffic in the 1800s. The remains are still used to bring water into Newport.

Both the 'Mon and Brec' and the Llangollen canals are examples of waterways built to transport important minerals such as coal, limestone and agricultural goods to market, through narrow river valleys. They wind along the sides, using high aqueducts to cross over when the contours dictate.

Plan your trip according to the wind and the weather as the canal is fairly exposed high up above the river valley, and the wind can cause problems for paddlers. You could paddle 'out and back' from Brecon, which would save doing a shuttle, or you can follow the one way trip described. It is 30km to Gilwern but this would be a long day's paddle, or there are shorter trips; 7.5km to the river aqueduct and back, 22km to Talybont-on-Usk and back (this avoids the Ashford Tunnel), and 33km to Llangynidr and back, avoiding the five Llangynidr locks.

The Monmouthshire and Brecon Canal

The canal opened in 1812 to transport coal, iron ore, iron and lime. It was supplied by tram roads which came down to the wharves at Llanfoist and Llangattock. With the advent of the railways, however, profits declined. The Monmouthshire Canal bought the waterway in 1865, and in 1880 it was sold to the Great Western Railway. The Newport end was closed in the late 1800s for the development of the docks, but it continued to be used as a water supply. Another part of this canal system can be found near Newport. The Crumlin Branch left at Malpas on the outskirts of Newport and climbed up to Crumlin in the Ebbw Vale. It survived until 1949.

To view this waterway, leave the M4 at Junction 27, and follow the B4591 to the outskirts of Cefn, from where the '14 Locks' are signposted. These and the visitor centre are well worth visiting. Today twelve out of eighteen kilometres north to Pontywaun (7.5km) are in water, with restoration planned by one of the canal trusts. Most of the 14 locks are derelict, but the rise of the canal through a densely wooded area is very atmospheric and worth the walk. There is a good path along the side of the canal. The canal then winds on a contour through Rogerstone, Ty-Sign and Risca to Crosskeys and Pontywaun. The latter stretch has a boat service at weekends.

Water level

The water level is constant as it is a maintained canal, but it is shallow all the way.

Campsites

There are sites near Brecon, just north of the canal, and one at Crickhowell on the left bank of the River Usk, just upstream from the bridge.

Access

Brecon Canal Basin – SO 048 281

Pencelli Bridge – SO 093 249

White Hart Bridge, Talybont-on-Usk – SO 114 225

Ashford Tunnel start (B4558 runs along the canal) – SO 122 217

Ashford Tunnel exit – SO 123 214

Llangynidr Lock No. 5 – SO 138 198

Llangynidr Lock No. 1 – SO 147 199

Llangynidr Bridge (parking near River Usk) – SO 152 200

Llyncelyn Bridge (B4558 crosses over river, parking nearby) – SO 185 193

Llangattock Quay (near Crickhowell) – SO 207 172

Gilwern Canal Basin and marina – SO 243 146

The marina and wharves are reached by taking a side road to the right up a steep hill just after entering Gilwern on the main road. Once the canal bridge is reached, a right turn gives access along the canal to parking.

Description

At the pleasant Brecon basin, there is a theatre, and a pay and display car park just over the road. The canal runs in a straight line behind houses, parallel with the original main A40 road. The first single lock is after 3km, at Brynich, and this is followed by a very sharp bend to the right to take the canal over the River Usk on a stone aqueduct. The 'Mon and Brec' then winds along a contour on the south side of the Usk Valley. There are several small villages, most with canalside pubs, but no more towns for the rest of the trip.

Llanfrynach is near, on the right, and then Pencelli. The canal passes under the B road which then follows the canal for miles. The winding Usk is clearly visible below in its flood plain. Talybont-on-Usk is next, with a lifting bridge, and the Ashford Tunnel (343m long) is soon after. As you enter the tunnel, the end is just a dot of light in the distance.

The valley narrows, and there is plenty of woodland. Just as the large village of Llangynidr (17km) comes into sight, there are 4 locks close together; **portage** on the left bank. The canal winds over a small river valley on an aqueduct, and then comes the next **portage**, of

a fifth lock. After this, there is a canal basin used for mooring boats, a very useful point to have a stop and walk down the steep hill to the fine stone bridge over the River Usk. The river here is one of the more famous whitewater kayaking stretches in Wales, and worth seeing in high water.

The canal winds its way back to the B road, and before the road crosses the canal, there are several parking places by the canal. You could start here if not wishing to paddle from Brecon, and enjoy this beautiful wooded part of the waterway, high above the Glanusk Park Estate. Llangattock village is next (24.5km) and the canal takes a large anti-clockwise loop around the village. The small market town of Crickhowell is not far away, on the other side of the Usk.

For the last part of this trip, the canal makes its way towards the river again, and joins the A4077 road, which remains alongside all the way into Gilwern for the last 3km. The large marina and turning point at Gilwern are just before the aqueduct over the River Clydach, where the canal is high up, with views over the countryside.

Index

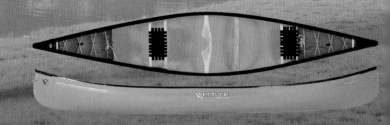